Ethica Thomistica

Ralph McInerny

Ethica Thomistica

The Moral Philosophy of Thomas Aquinas

REVISED EDITION

The Catholic University of America Press
Washington, D.C.

The paper used in this publication meets the minimum requirements of
American National Standards for Information Science—Permanence of Paper for
Printed Library materials, ANSI Z39.48–1984.

∞

Library of Congress Cataloging-in-Publication Data
McInerny, Ralph M.
    Ethica thomistica : the moral philosophy of Thomas Aquinas / by
Ralph McInerny. — Rev. ed.
        p. cm.
    Includes bibliographical references.
    ISBN 0-8132-0897-1 (pbk. : alk. paper)
        1. Thomas, Aquinas, Saint, 1225?–1274—Ethics.   2. Ethics—
History.   3. Christian ethics—History—Middle Ages, 600–1500.
    I. Title.
    B765.T54M392   1997
    171'.2'092-dc21   97-11164

For Alasdair MacIntyre

Contents

Preface

This little book has been out of print for several years, and it is pleasant to hear that it has been missed. It is about as elementary as a book on ethics can ethically be, but for all that it is true, although not the whole truth. By which I mean that much more could be said, not that what is said here would need to be unsaid.

As the Preface to the original edition explains, this book arose from an assignment to lay before a summer institute the way Thomas Aquinas did moral philosophy, in its broad lines. My effort was well-received and, when it eventually became a book, many found it useful as a capsule statement of Thomistic Ethics. I am delighted that it is to be granted a new lease on life.

It should be said that Thomas had no sense that he was doing ethics, or indeed philosophy, in a personal way, or in one way as opposed to others, at least if such pluralism were taken to be radical. Thomas did philosophy, not Thomistic philosophy, just as Aristotle did philosophy and was not intent on fabricating an unusual and personal system.

Modern philosophy sometimes looks like one effort after another to be original, to be different, to go where no man has gone before. Greek philosophy began as verse and became prose; modern philosophy began in Latin and then turned to the various vernaculars and to the nationalism they often involved. Once there had been simply philosophy, and a lingua franca in which to express it; now there was French Philosophy, German Philosophy, British Philosophy, and so on. And within each of these philoso-

X Ethica Thomistica

phies, every philosopher seemed intent on fashioning a *patois* quite different from ordinary French or German or English.

Poets, it is thought, are under obligation to be original and difficult; their readers must submit to them and see the world as they do. One can argue this assumption, or at least modify it, as T. S. Eliot did in "Tradition and the Individual Talent," but we now see this assumption being openly applied to philosophers, who are urged to become "strong poets." Self-assertive, that is, there being nothing else to assert, it seems.

The seeds for such nonsense were present at the beginning, when Descartes fashioned what he called Methodic Doubt. Doubt was necessary if Descartes was to know that he knew anything for sure. Whatever passed successfully through the fire of doubt could lay claim to being an item of knowledge. This is a familiar story, but notice a fundamental assumption of it. Until and unless I subject my views to methodic doubt, I have no right to say I know anything. Now, methodic doubt is something philosophers do—apparently not before Descartes, however, which is not insignificant—and this means that people who do not have time or talent for philosophy cannot be numbered among those who know.

It is doubtful whether Descartes, by all accounts a nice fellow, a good Catholic who attended a Jesuit college, intended this elitist consequence. But there it is. What the mass of mankind say is of no epistemic value in the quest for truth.

On the other hand, the assumption of a Thomas Aquinas or an Aristotle is that everybody already knows things for sure about the world and himself. There are truths common to everyone insofar as they are human. These truths are not deliverances of philosophy but are naturally known and presupposed by philosophy. Philosophy starts from these naturally known truths and tries to push beyond them, not to call them into question but to place its anchor in them. When the philosopher can no longer explain what he means in terms of what everybody already knows, it is the philosopher who loses, not the mass of mankind.

A good deal of the strangeness of philosophy since Descartes can be traced to this elitist conception of philosophy and its implicit disdain for your Uncle George. On the classical assumption, philosophers will have their distinctive voices, their differing styles, but their addressee is in principle anyone, and their subject is reality, not the lint to be found in their navels. Such reflections influence what one thinks he is doing when asked to give a summary of Thomistic Ethics. The way to read this book is to ask whether it jibes with what everyone knows. If it does not, I have failed to present Thomas faithfully, and you should burn this book and turn to Thomas. Such revisions as have been made are aimed at staving off this failure. Chapter Three has received the most reshaping. Previously, I criticized the views of Germain Grisez and John Finnis *et sequaces eorum,* but I have come to think that this is not the place to do that. As those two admirable gentlemen understand, this is not a recantation.

Notre Dame, Indiana
January, 1997

Ethica Thomistica

1. Morality and Human Life

When St. Thomas says that the subject matter of moral philosophy is human action—human actions are moral actions and vice versa—he captures our sense that the moral or ethical pervades human life, but he also leaves us wondering how something so broad can constitute the object of a particular inquiry. Some light is cast on this problem when we consider his conception of human action. A human act is one that is conscious, deliberate, and free, something for which we are answerable. "Why did you do that?" "What should I do?" But surely there are answers to such questions —"There was a man on third" and "Try an eight iron," say—that we would hesitate to call moral or assign to the province of ethics.

Reed Armstrong making a statue is engaged in responsible action, yet we would distinguish both the knowledge embodied in his activity and the reflection on such activity by himself and others from moral philosophy. The sculptor, the engineer, the angler, the scholar, the shortstop are all engaged in human action, yet it would be odd to call reflection on their deeds moral philosophy. Has Thomas cast too wide a net?

A human action is undertaken for a purpose, with an end in view. Its appraisal will take into account the means employed to achieve the end. An attempt to open a lock with a paper key will usually be regarded as a bad way to go about achieving the end in view. Means are ill or well adapted to the purpose for which one acts. Another appraisal of action bears on the end, goal or purpose itself. Ends themselves, and not just the means of attaining them, can be assessed as good or bad.

1

St. Thomas, like his philosophical mentor Aristotle, seems at the outset to deprive himself of any basis for discriminating between good and bad ends. He says that every action is undertaken with a view to some end *and* that the end has the character of the good. But if every action has a purpose or end and every end is good, it looks as if every action must be a good one, if good action is action which aims at the good.

"Good" here means perfective of or fulfilling of the agent. I want something I do not have because having it is preferable to not having it. Hence I pursue it. Latent in any action is the belief that its end is perfective or fulfilling of the one acting. That the pursuit achieves its end is the good the agent seeks. But how in this perspective can there be bad actions? Thomas and Aristotle provide an answer by distinguishing between real and apparent goods.

A real good is something I pursue as perfective or fulfilling of me and that really would perfect or fulfill me if I had it. An apparent good, by contrast, is an end pursued as perfective or fulfilling of me that, if had, really would not perfect or fulfill me. Let us say that you come upon me seated at table. Before me is a heaping bowl of carpet tacks. I pour low fat milk over them, sprinkle them with a sugar substitute, and bring a spoonful toward my mouth. Orad, as they say in crossword puzzles. You give a cry and stay my hand. "Why would you want to eat carpet tacks?" you reasonably inquire. "I have been told that I need more iron in my diet," say I. You, in your role of tacks assessor, explain to me that eating tacks is not the way to achieve my goal. Your assumption is that I want more iron in my diet in order to regain my health and restore roses to my cheeks. Unquestioned in your intervention would be that health is good and that iron is a constituent of health. The end is thus left untouched by your criticism. Of course I might have responded to your question with a sigh, given you an abbreviated account of my recent travails and said that I wanted to shuffle off this mortal coil. The internal hemorrhaging promised by the consumption of a bowl of carpet tacks seemed to my troubled mind an effective way to achieve my end. What would you say to that?

Obviously if my end is my end, so to say, I will be in logical difficulty in maintaining that my fulfillment or perfection consists in my not being at all and in the internal bleeding that will bring this about. The nonexistence of the human agent can scarcely qualify as the good, perfection, or fulfillment of the human agent. Let us say that I am surprised in the act of persuading or even forcing a fellow diner to consume the bowl of tacks. My end now is the extermination of another, perhaps the pushy fellow who stayed my hand and asked me why I had not eschewed a tacks free lunch. I am proceeding on the assumption that his ceasing to be will be better for me than his continuance in existence. Can reducing the number of my tablemates by one in this way really be perfective or fulfilling of me? That I can have such a goal and pursue it as good is surely possible, but could my pursuit and achievement of that goal really be good? As we shall see, one of the tasks of the moral philosopher, according to Thomas, is to discover the criteria that will enable him to show that such an end is only apparently, not really, good.

But what of all those human actions that do not seem to be moral ones at all and whose appraisal appeals to scientific, aesthetic, culinary, and other criteria? If not all human actions are susceptible of a moral appraisal, how can Thomas maintain an equivalence between human action and moral action? Let us take a case.

Thaddeus Skillen is engaged in research aimed at making lung cancer a mere memory for the race. We come upon him in his lab thoughtfully smoking a mentholated cigarette as he inspects the cloudy contents of a beaker. Mice scamper in the cages behind him. There is the fetid smell we associate with creativity. A massive apparatus covers an entire table, and there is the muted and, to Thaddeus, musical murmur of bubbling liquids, the faint hiss of escaping gases, an ambience which appeals to the thwarted Madame Curie in the observer. Skillen has infected mice with the

substance he now contemplates. A wondrous, not quite trium-
phant smile disturbs his bearded countenance. The reports are in.
An assistant has just told him that a previously cancerous mouse
has achieved a clean bill of health as the result of injections of this
fluid. Thaddeus Skillen has perfected a cure for lung cancer.

Good for him? Of course. May he receive a Nobel prize. Let
us be the first to congratulate the potential laureate. But is our
praise of Skillen moral praise? Is our appraisal of what he has done
appraisal of moral action? Not necessarily. We might be taken to
be saying simply that he has performed his scientific work well.
Surely that can be disengaged from a moral appraisal of his acts.
This would be quite clear if we were to widen our perspective and
add a negative moral appraisal to our positive appraisal of his work
as a scientist.

Imagine Frau Skillen and all the little Skillens reduced to skin
and bones by the singlemindedness with which the eponymous
Skillen has pursued a cure for lung cancer. The cupboard is bare,
the house is unheated, shoeless little Skillens wander unloved
and morose through the cheerless rooms. Viewed in this wider
perspective, Skillen comes under another appraisal that conflicts
with our praise for his research. This prompts us to take a closer
look around the lab. To our alarm, we notice that some of the
cages contain human beings and they are treated no better than
germ-free mice. Our eye is drawn to a pair of white-knuckled
hands on the window sill, and we find one of Skillen's assistants
clinging there, about to fall, crying for help, his plight ignored by
our scientist.

Such everyday examples suggest that human actions can be
appraised in several ways—internally, as we might say, and exter-
nally or, better, comprehensively, that is, morally. The non-moral
appraisal of human action will thus seem to be a foreshortened
perspective. Of course, we can assess the deeds of a golfer, cook,
accountant by appealing to the criteria of golf, cooking, and ac-
countancy. But all such acts can also be appraised morally. Are
they, in the round, comprehensively, conducive to the good of

the agent, his private good, and the good he shares with others of his kind? No human action can escape this wider appraisal although any human action can also be appraised non-morally. To be sure, no set of non-moral criteria will have the comprehensive range of the moral. There are some who do not golf or cook and, while we may pity them, we do not blame them.

The pervasiveness of the moral, the fact that human action and moral action are identical, has obvious implications for the question frequently asked, and not only by philosophers: Why should I be moral? The question may seem to suggest that a person may or may not choose to act from a moral point of view. For St. Thomas this would mean that a person may or may not choose to perform moral actions. But if human actions are just as such moral and if one cannot not act, then, simply by dint of being a human agent, one is a moral agent. It is necessarily the case that a human person who acts is engaged in moral action and thus subject to moral appraisal.

Needless to say, one does not necessarily perform human actions well, and if the question were taken to mean: Why should I act well?, then of course it points to a basic option. One is free to act either well or badly, and to choose to act well is something one may or may not do. Has one who chooses not to act well rejected morality and rendered moral appraisal of what he does impertinent and irrelevant? Would not moral appraisals of his deeds be alien, since they embody an outlook that others may accept but he has rejected? Not quite. If human acts are just as such moral, they are as such either good or bad. Let us speak of moral$_1$ to cover human acts both good and bad. Then moral$_2$ can be taken to mean those human acts which are performed well, i.e. good human acts. Every human act is necessarily moral$_1$, but not necessarily moral$_2$. It is a matter of necessity, not choice, that any act I perform is moral$_1$. It is a matter of choice, not necessity, that an action of mine is moral$_2$. The question "Why should I be moral?" can only mean, as far as Thomas is concerned, "Why should I be moral$_2$?"

We will not immediately seek an answer to that question. Let us rather return to considering whether someone who chooses not to act well, whether episodically or as a matter of policy, can regard the question only as someone else's question, posed from a viewpoint other than his own. I think Thomas would rightly reject this interpretation as unreal. The commitment or intention to act well is embodied in each and every action anyone performs. If human action is purposive, undertaken with an end in view, and the end has the character of good, then no matter what I do, I do it with the intention of doing what is perfective or fulfilling of me. This is as true when I act badly as it is when I act well. When I act badly I am pursuing something which is only apparently good, perhaps because it is a real good pursued in the wrong way, at the wrong time, etc. But I can only pursue it as what is perfective of me. Perfective does not, of course, mean heroic virtue or the perfection of which Jesus speaks. *(Be perfect as your heavenly Father is perfect.)* If I am mistaken about what I pursue, if it really isn't fulfilling of me, that latent, implicit intention provides an intrinsic criterion according to which my action can be appraised. Thus the question, "Why should I be moral$_2$?" can be answered: Because that is already the intention with which you act. The question does not arise from an alien viewpoint; it is the rock bottom assumption of my acting at all.

The human agent cannot not act. This does not mean that I am compelled to do this action or that, but rather that I must perform some action or other. (Imagine deciding not to act for the rest of the week.) Any action that I perform is just as such moral$_1$. Actions can be appraised from a number, a countless number, of viewpoints other than the moral, but each and every human act can be appraised morally, that is, as done because it is thought to be conducive to what is truly perfective and fulfilling of the agent. Some acts can be appraised as those of a golfer; some as those of an accountant; some as those of a scientist. And on and on. But all these acts can also be appraised morally. That is, all the things that a human person consciously, purposely, and freely does are moral acts. Thus, while a human agent is just as such a moral agent, his actions are susceptible to appraisals that appeal both to intrinsic or narrow criteria and to comprehensive moral criteria. The moral order is as broad as the scope of human action itself, encompassing theoretical and practical matters insofar as the human agent freely and accountably addresses himself to them.

This conception of human action and of the scope of morality can give rise to a bad picture of human life broadly taken, and Thomas is intent on avoiding that bad picture. It has been said that human life is a book in which we set out to write one story and end by writing another. This does not simply mean that earlier I set out to do such-and-such and later changed my mind and decided instead to do this-or-that. The observation has a far deeper significance.

The story of a human life always involves far more than a person's responsible moral actions. By the time a person is capable of an interest in moral philosophy, he has already acquired a complex personal history. When you look back upon your past life, you will doubtless find it impossible to see it as just a chain of actions of the kind we have been discussing. Of course, you intended A and then you intended B. You chose, decided, thought about the future, did this and that, and all these things count as free, conscious and responsible deeds. They are the things you set out to do. But every human life is a very complicated mixture of the intended and unintended, and it is not possible to sort them out in such a way that all the intended acts would make up a set completely independent of what just happened to me.

Take a simple instance. Imagine that going to see the Cubs play in Wrigley Field is a rational thing to do, at least in the sense that a person can deliberately do such a thing. Let us say that I decide to go to Chicago and take in a game. On the Indiana Toll Road I have a flat tire, and a car pulls over to give me aid. Behind the wheel is a very attractive young lady whose name, I quickly learn, is Fifi LaRue, perhaps a stage name. She offers to take me to the next oasis. I accept. As we drive away her tawny tresses are tossed by the errant breeze. I experience pleasant palpitations of the kind associated with infatuation along with concupiscent complications. At the oasis, prior to arranging for the wrecker to go for my car, I ask Fifi to have a cup of coffee with me. When we enter the restaurant, a siren goes off, bells ring, bright lights turn on, and cameras roll. With Fifi on my arm I am the fifteen millionth customer to patronize the tollway restaurant. The story is carried on national television. My wife turns on the evening news and sees footage of me making my historic entry with a radiant Fifi on my arm. Among the prizes that I win is a trip to Bermuda, and it is there, on the golden sands, bronzing in the sunshine, that my wife and I are finally reconciled. My arm is healing nicely, the swelling around my eyes is going down, the future looks bright. The child who is the fruit of our reconciliation. . . . But enough. Such a story can go on and on. That's life. Indeed it is. The Cubs lose 11–1.

In any such account as this, we can discern actions of the kind Thomas calls moral, but we also recognize events that, while connected with my choices, were not intended by me. I decided to go to Chicago, and I happened to have a flat tire. I accepted a lift from Fifi with no idea of what lay ahead. I invited her for a cup of coffee, but I did not intend to be on national TV. I intended to enter the restaurant, but I did not intend to be the winner of all those prizes. When I acted, I acted in a set of circumstances that were in part a result of previous choices and in part the unintended consequences of those choices. Human action, defined as purposive, undertaken with an end in view, is always open to fortuitous consequences, and for those I am not held accountable, though, of course, as my wife explains, I am responsible for what I next do in the circumstances that then present themselves.

Thomas defines a fortuitous effect of my purposive actions as unlooked-for, rare, and significant. The human agent is always prey to luck, good and bad, but one gets neither credit nor blame for such effects of his decisions. The story of a life can hardly be told without mention of the adventitious, of what *happened* to me when I acted. If I am the cause of the unintended as well as the intended effects of my choices, I am clearly not the cause of each kind of effect in the same way. If I drive a golf ball and suddenly a cart darts into the fairway and my ball strikes the driver on the head and kills him, I can say that the ball went an uninterrupted two hundred yards because I intended that it should, and I can say that the imprudent driver died because I drove my ball, but I am not the cause of his death in the same way that I am the cause of my ball's going a certain distance. If I had foreseen my ball striking him, I would have refrained from driving when I did. But this has never happened to me before. I have never killed a fellow golfer in all my checkered career. My opponent would reasonably regard me as eccentric if I said that I would not drive just now because of a number of logically possible consequences of my doing so. A low-flying aircraft, say a stealth bomber, might be brought down by my Spalding 3. There are many reasons why I ought not golf, perhaps, but this is scarcely one of them. A certain amount of prudent caution is advisable before teeing up and swinging away, but no amount of caution can forestall the unforeseeable. For that matter, if I should dally on the tee because I am oppressed by thoughts of what unimaginable consequences might follow from my hitting the ball, I should be made aware that my decision not to act is itself fraught with possible menace. A robin kicks from its nest on an overhanging branch an unhatched egg. the egg strikes my partner on the nose and, in his surprise and consternation, he lurches wildly, swinging his club and catching me behind the ear. In a quince, I lie bloody and inert upon the greensward.

Life is like that. Human agents are always cause of more than they intend and often of consequences that are significantly good or evil. Such results are related to moral decision, but they are not per se the consequences of it. Of course, if a pattern emerges, I must take it into account. If every time I hit a golf ball someone is struck by it, I would find it progressively more difficult to see this as an accidental result of what I am doing. I might give up the game, perhaps even voluntarily.

Such reflections enable us to distinguish between the good and evil that are qualities of my actions and for which I am held accountable, and the good and evil that may befall me as a result of acting but for which I am not held accountable. Søren Kierkegaard wished to distinguish between ethics and history on the basis of these two senses of good and evil, arguing, much as Tolstoy would at the end of *War and Peace,* that historical significance depends far more on what happens to people than on what they intend. In any case, the distinction between the two senses of good and evil is clear enough.

The distinction enables us to see why St. Thomas, having defined human action as he does, nonetheless holds that we have a most imperfect control over how our lives, broadly conceived, turn out. His religious faith and ours enables us to hold that events that are unintended by human agents even though they are consequences of responsible choices are not through and through unintended. No event in the created order escapes the providence of God. Thus it is useful for us to ask why something happened to us, why we have been lucky or unlucky. The answer cannot presume to be definitive but may nonetheless have significance for how we view our lives.

Few things are more conducive to the realization that we are creatures who have only an imperfect control over our lives than our constant openness to the unexpected and unintended consequences of our deeds. Greek tragedy, as analyzed by Aristotle, relies heavily on the fortuitous event. A man marries a widow not knowing that she is in truth his mother. What he intended to do in marrying her and what he actually did by intending it are very different things and, because incest is so horrible, the protagonist, when he learns the true nature of his deed, feels that he must make retribution. But his guilt cannot be moral guilt, since he did not intend to do what he did. Some have spoken of this as existential guilt, meaning perhaps that, being the kinds of agents we are, we cannot escape our fate of unintentionally causing evils we do not intend. But then in fairness we should speak of existential merit too, to cover those good effects that we do not intend but that result unexpectedly from our doing what we mean to do.

These reflections are meant to allay the fear that St. Thomas, by equating human action and moral action, takes human life to be a seamless whole made up only of rational choices of which the results are always intended and must be referred to the agent as to their responsible cause. Life is far more complicated than that. Indeed, within the context of these considerations, the moral order, earlier taken to be pervasive, can come to seem a small area of illumination within a circumambient darkness. The moral order is not so wide as human life even though human action is equated with moral action. If Thomas quite sensibly concentrates on human action—the conscious, purposive things we do—as the subject of moral philosophy, he is fully aware that there are more things in heaven and earth, and in our lives, than are dreamt of in our philosophy.

2. The Good for Man

When St. Thomas says that every human action is undertaken for some purpose, with an end in view, and that the end has the character of the good, he is echoing Aristotle. Aristotle held not only that each human act has its particular goal and end but also that there is an overriding ultimate end for the sake of which each human action is undertaken. Because of Thomas's dependence on Aristotle, it seems right first to consider the great pagan philosopher's teaching and then to go on to Thomas's development of the concept of ultimate end.

ARISTOTLE

In this section I am concerned with three interrelated and overlapping questions: What does Aristotle mean by "end" and "ultimate end"? Where and how does he show that man has an ultimate end? In what sense is the ultimate end one? I shall confine myself almost exclusively to Book One of the *Nicomachean Ethics* in seeking answers to these questions.

"Every art and every inquiry, and similarly every action and pursuit, is thought to aim at some good; and for this reason the good has rightly been declared to be that at which all things aim." Thus begins the *Nicomachean Ethics*. The sentence attempts, one might say, a swift inventory of human acts or deeds. They are all as such teleological, undertaken for some purpose, done with an end in view. Furthermore, a first determination of the meaning of 'good' is given. The good is the aim, purpose or end of an action, where, of course, 'good' means the good for man since we are speaking of human deeds.

This is a startling way to begin a treatise on ethics. If every human action aims at an end, and if the end and the good are one, then each and every human action is, as human action, good. In order to escape this leveling consequence, Aristotle needs some criterion whereby he can distinguish between real and apparent goods. How will he find one?

His procedure is roughly this. If any action is undertaken with an end in view, with an eye to some good, what is sought as good is taken to be perfective of the agent. That is, the not-doing or not-having is less perfective than the doing or having. One seeks what one does not have and seeks it because having it is preferable, is the completion of a capacity, the fulfillment of a need. Whatever a human person does or seeks is done or sought under this broad assumption. But not everything so sought is really perfective of the agent. Thus Aristotle proceeds on the assumption that knowledge of the kind of agent we are will provide a criterion for distinguishing among the things we seek those that are truly perfective of us from those that are not. Hence the traditional talk of real and apparent goods.

Aristotle characteristically clarifies the issues involved by appeal to artistic or technical activities. Just as the human artifact is the basic metaphor he employs to speak of natural objects, so here, and even more fittingly, he anchors the meaning of terms in human making before turning explicitly to human doing. No one can doubt the pedagogical utility of this procedure, but here as elsewhere we must be extremely careful lest the aid become an impediment. "But a certain difference is found among ends; some are activities, others are products *(erga)* apart from the activities that produce them. Where there are ends apart from the actions, it is the nature of the products to be better than the activities." Though it is not quite so neat as this, I take the distinction between product-beyond-action and action-as-end to be an adumbration of the distinction between art *(techne)* and prudence *(phronesis).* If the former casts light on the latter, it can also mislead, not least when we are speaking of ends and means. In the case of art, activity is a means relative to the product as end, so that in art the aim is the good or perfection of the artifact. In the case of man as doer, action is not a means but the end. This remains true even if we say that action of a certain kind is that whereby the agent becomes good. His goodness here is a disposition to perform acts of the kind in question in appropriate future circumstances.

"Now, as there are many actions, arts and sciences, their ends are also many." This remark reminds us, should we need reminding, that the opening sentence of the *Nicomachean Ethics,* if true, tells us something true of each and every human deed, whether art, science, or choice, but the unity of the remark is that of generality. That is, some one thing is true of everything we do. If every action aims at some end, this does not entail that there is some such end at which all actions aim. Always willing to be explicit, Aristotle gives a list: the end of the medical art is health, that of shipbuilding a vessel, that of strategy victory, that of economics wealth. And so on. If any game is a recreational activity, this truth does not inform us of the immense variety of kinds of games. If any action has an end, this truth cannot substitute for the immense variety of ends. The picture that thus emerges is this: While we can soar above the arena of human activity and say that whatever a human person does aims at an end, when we descend we seem faced with the prospect of piecemeal analysis of now this end, now that, now the next, and so on *ad infinitum.*

But there may be another way of gathering ends, of unifying actions in clusters, a way that is not that of predicable universality but of subordination and superordination. (Of course the Porphyrean tree, the classical image of greater and lesser universality, also employs the language of subordination and superordination— man subordinated to animal, animal superordinated to man—so that the task may be seen as one of distinguishing modalities of these terms.) How can actions or goods be clustered? "But where such arts fall under a single capacity . . . in all these the ends of the master arts are to be preferred to all the subordinate ends; for it is for the sake of the former that the latter are pursued." The end of bridle-making is bridles, of stirrup-making stirrups, of saddle-making saddles. These ends are for the sake of riding, of horsemanship, and horsemanship may be subordinated to military strategy, the art of war, whose end is victory. Activities and their ends can be subordinated to a further end that is superordinate. These prefixes should not be read in terms of greater or less predicable scope; the picture is not that of species subordinated to genus but of ends become means to a further end.

Having indicated (a) how we can say something that, while generally true of every action, leaves open the need to examine the special ends of particular actions or kinds of actions one at a time, and (b) that the sheer diversity of human teleological activity can be mastered somewhat by clustering actions when the ends of several are subordinate to the end of another activity, Aristotle next suggests that the second mode, if pursued, can lead to the grand sweep of the first mode. "If, then, there is some end of the things we do, which we desire for its own sake (everything else being desired for the sake of this), and if we do not choose everything for the sake of something else (at that rate, the process would go on to infinity, so that our desire would be empty and vain), clearly this must be the good and the chief good."

What is the force of this passage? If we were to ignore the second parenthetical remark, it would seem to he a mere hypothesis, a subjunctive, perhaps an optative, remark. If we take the second parenthetical remark into account, however, we seem to have an argument to the effect that there must be such an ultimate superordinating end of all we do.

Even if one were to take the quoted passage as a hypothesis, one would have to say that it is soon rendered categorical by appeal to two quite different sorts of facts. In the immediate sequel, we find Aristotle proceeding in the following way. If there were such an ultimate end, knowledge of it would be of the greatest usefulness. Like archers who have a target to aim at, we would then be in a position to aim in the right direction.

Furthermore, if there should be such an ultimate superordinating end, concern with it would fall to politics, the master art of human affairs. It is this observation that can be seen as leading Aristotle forth from his hypothetical reverie. When we consider the political order, we find that such an ultimate end is presupposed. Aristotle has in mind the statesman in his role as legislator. Laws are passed concerning every conceivable human activity; no overt human behavior seems to escape the possible purview of the law, if only because a law might be passed saying that such-and-such an activity is not to be interfered with. If law is proscriptive, regulative, permissive, or protective, it would seem that in principle any and every human activity can be covered by it. For this to be possible, however, the lawmaker must have some vantage point, some end in view, some good in mind, when he thus takes into account the whole of human activity. And would this not be some ultimate superordinating end to which particular ends of particular activities are subordinated? Thus, whether or not the passage is understood as an argument to the effect that there must be an ultimate end of human activity, it is clear that, later on, by appeal to law, Aristotle asserts that men do recognize such an ultimate end.

There is another, so to speak factual, appeal that Aristotle makes to turn his hypothetical into a categorical. He says that there is at least verbal agreement among men that there is an ultimate end, verbal agreement because we have a name for it: happiness *(eudaimonia)*. This then is one way of construing the quoted passage. If there were an ultimate superordinating end of human action, it would be our chief good. But both legislation and the way men speak of happiness suggest a recognition of such an ultimate end. Ergo, etc.

Nonetheless, friend and foe alike have taken the passage in question to be an argument, not a hypothesis, and the second parenthetical remark supports this interpretation. If there were no ultimate end, our desire would be vain and empty. That is, if human action is not to be nonsense, there must be an ultimate end. Presuming this to be an argument, how good an argument is it? Here are some standard objections to it:

1. Aristotle is here misled by the linear analogy of subordinate and superordinate ends. Real life revolves in lazy circles. I want A in order that B and B in order that C and C in order that A. That is, I exercise in order to be healthy in order to work to earn a vacation in Florida where I will loll in the sun and exercise in order to be healthy in order to fulfill the duties of my job, etc., etc., so that what was for-something-else may later in its turn become the aim of its erstwhile aim.

2. No doubt there are some people who sacrifice everything to some one dominant passion of their lives, but why put so high a premium on a particular psychological type? Henry James and Erle Stanley Gardiner were driven men, everything in their lives subordinated to a single-minded purpose and deriving its importance therefrom, but not everyone is like that. There are more pleasant types—you and I—who seek to orchestrate their aims in such a way that no one of them achieves dominance over the others. What we want is a harmony of ends rather than one overriding purpose.

3. Aristotle is guilty of a foolish fallacy. He passes from "All chains must end somewhere." to "There is somewhere that all chains end." Or from "Every road comes to a stop someplace." to "There is some one place where all roads stop." Rome, perhaps.

One's first reaction to these objections is that Aristotle ought not be open to them—call this the pious reaction. If the notion of ultimate end makes sense, it ought not do so at the expense of what the objectors remind us of. As for the third objection, if it has force, it amounts to an Aristotelian objection to Aristotle. The point it makes is precisely the one Aristotle made in the first chapter of the *Nicomachean Ethics*. The common truth that every action has an end is not an argument for a common end of all actions. Has the introduction of what we have called the clustering of actions, of subordination and superordination, clouded Aristotle's mind on this point and in so short a space?

As to the second parenthetical remark in the passage under discussion, it could be said that it too goes against the grain of the first chapter of Book One of the *Nicomachean Ethics*. Why should we think that, in the absence of an ultimate end, our desire would be vain and empty? An end is an end. If this action has an end, this saves our desire from being vain and empty. So too with the next one and the next and so on. It is not its subordination to a further end that makes an end an end in the first place. Without such subordination it remains an end. The parenthetical remark seems to treat any particular end as if it were for-the-sake-of-something in the sense that it is not sought for its own sake. But that would make every end that is less than the putative ultimate end merely instrumental, not desirable in itself. All such ends would be like bitter medicine taken for the sake of health. What is Aristotle trying to say?

The way out of the woods here is to see that the examples Aristotle brought forward to illustrate what he meant by subordination and superordination, helpful as they are, can produce a bad picture. The examples show how several particular activities can be subordinated to the end of another particular activity. But surely Aristotle is not suggesting that there is some particular act to whose end all others are subordinable. What then can he mean by ultimate end?

Perhaps this. We know what bricklaying is and what its end is; so too with plumbing, fiddling, teaching French irregular verbs, ice-fishing, playing Scrabble, and so on. But all of these are human acts. If there are criteria for fiddling well and fishing well, are there none for performing human action well? Needless to say, this is a surprising direction for Aristotle to take. We know how to go about ascribing actions and/or products to a man qua fiddler or qua fisher or qua geometer, but what would it mean to ascribe an activity to man qua man? Must we not simply say that human acts are the things humans do, on the model of the familiar phrase that philosophy is what philosophers do? To be sure, the latter is a go-away or dismissive definition. That is, it indicates unwillingness to give a definition, and it is vulnerable to some such sorites as this: Philosophy is what philosophers do; Socrates is a philosopher; Socrates can shimmy like my sister Kate; philosophers can shimmy like my sister Kate. The go-away definition has a comeback here, even if my sister Kate is herself a philosopher. Not every philosopher can shimmy, let alone like my sister Kate. But how can we move from "Human acts are what humans do" to "do qua human"? What conceivable contrast could we have in mind?

Another surprising feature of this apparent turn in Aristotle's argument is that it takes him right back to the opening sentence of the *Nicomachean Ethics*. But in returning to his opening remark, Aristotle now treats it intensively, so to say, rather than extensively. These technical adverbs can be explained by having recourse to the famous seventh chapter of Book One of the *Nicomachean Ethics*.

The seventh chapter begins with a brief summary of the first and second chapters. The good is related to actions as their end. There are as many goods as there are actions. The actions in question are human actions. Are there criteria for an action's being human as there are criteria for particular actions being the kind they are, i.e., fiddling, fishing, etc.? If we could find a criterion for human action as such, we would be able to speak of the human good, i.e., the goal of human actions as human. Let us put the matter schematically.

Let *x* and *y* be human actions. Then

    a. both *x* and *y* aim at goods or ends;
    b. the end of *x* differs from the end of *y*;
    c. doing *x* well or badly is read from the end at which it aims; so too with *y*;
    d. doing *x* well differs from doing *y* well;
    e. if doing *x* well and doing *y* well are both instances of good human activity, can we give an account of "acting humanly well" that is neither (i) another way of saying "doing *x*

well" nor (ii) the conjunction of "doing *x* well" and "doing *y* well" and "doing *n* well"?

    f. such an account of "acting humanly well" would be what is meant by the ultimate superordinate end.

    A terminological point. The human good, man's chief good, is variously expressed as happiness *(eudaimonia)*, acting well *(eu prattein)*, living well *(eu zen)*, that for the sake of which *(hou kharin)*, and ultimate end *(ariston teleion)*. These terms do not mean some particular good among others (cf. *EN* 1097b17–19). Thus, the human good cannot be the end of a particular action, of some one action distinct from all other human actions. The ultimate good, then, must be that which makes the countless goods at which human actions aim human goods. We know how to describe the end of man qua flutist, qua fiddler, qua fisher. How can we describe the end or good of the human agent qua human?

    "This might perhaps be given if we could first ascertain the function of man. For just as for a flute player, a sculptor, or any artist, and, in general, for all things that have a function or activity, the good and the 'well' is thought to reside in the function, so would it seem to be for man, if he has a function." The word 'function' here translates *ergon;* I say here advisedly since Aristotle used the word in the first chapter to designate the product-beyond-activity. It is clear that function explicates the qualocution. If you know what an activity aims at, you are thereby able to assess whether it is done well or badly. This is what is expressed in step e. of the above schema. Man's function would enable us to interpret the 'well' *(eu)* in the list of synonymous expressions given in the preceding paragraph. As it happens, Aristotle illustrates what he means by function by two quite different questions.

    1. Have the carpenter, then, and the tanner certain functions or activities, and has man none? Is he born without a function?

2. Or, as eye, hand, foot, and in general each of the parts evidently has a function, may one lay it down that man similarly has a function apart from all these? What can this function be?

Ad 1. This passage establishes the notion of function in the way we have been suggesting: man qua carpenter, man qua tanner, man qua harpist, man qua sculptor, etc. Such qua-locutions designate man from a particular activity which has its own end, good, or purpose, and the activity is assessed as well or badly done by reference to its end. If the human agent could be designated qua human, we would then be able to explicate the 'well' in 'acting well' *(eu prattein)* and in 'living well' *(eu zen)*.

Ad 2. This passage suggests the way to isolate human action as such, human life as such. Here we are given activities of parts of man (his eye, his hand, his foot) as opposed to particular human activities. The first passage can speak of 'function and action' *(ergon kai praxis)*, the second only of 'function' *(ergon)*. Further. the second passage mentions vital processes, manifestations of life, that can truly be predicated of man (e.g., a man sees, a man touches, a man walks) but that are not peculiar to him. The first passage treats human action extensively; the second shows how we can get at the notion of human action or human life intensively; that is, unpack it in such a way that we discover its formal note.

In search of an account of 'living humanly well,' Aristotle now suggests that there are types of vital activity that can truly be predicated of man, but not qua man. Think of the difference between "Socrates' beard is growing" and "Socrates is growing a beard." Aristotle puts it this way:

> Life seems to be common even to plants, but we are seeking what is peculiar to man. Let us exclude, therefore, the life of nutrition and growth.

The important word here is "common." Some vital activities that are found in man are also found in non-human beings; therefore they are not peculiar to man and cannot be the kind of activity or function we are seeking whose 'well' will be the human good.

> Next there would be a life of perception, but it also seems common even to the horse, the ox, and every animal.

This is reminiscent of the second illustration of what he means by *ergon* or function.

> There remains, then, an active life of the element that has a rational principle; of this, one part has such a principle in the sense of being obedient to one, the other in the sense of possessing and exercising thought.

Those vital activities of man that exhibit a rational principle pertain to man qua man. It is now clear that this account of activities of man qua man discriminates among activities that are truly predicated of him. Not all such activities are true of man as man because not all of them are peculiar to man. Only the activity or activities that are peculiar to man are true of him as such and are human activities *tout court*. Just as 'shimmying like my sister Kate' is not what philosophers do as philosophers, so growing, seeing, hearing, digesting, etc. do not pertain to man as man. These activities are no more restricted to men than 'shimmying like my sister Kate' is restricted to philosophers. We see, too, that in his first illustration of what he means by function, Aristotle is not distinguishing human action from fiddling, fishing, and flauting; rather he is after what each embodies in its way, namely, rational conscious activity.Some have found fault with Aristotle's search for a distinctively human activity. It has been objected that there are a number, perhaps a countless number, of things that only men do, such as writing sonnets, robbing banks, setting forest fires, and so on. This objection incorporates several mistakes. First, the objector fails to realize that his examples are precisely instances of the kind of activity that is peculiar to man. Second, the objection, when expanded, sometimes suggests that Aristotle thinks of 'acting rationally' as another item on a list that includes writing sonnets, robbing banks, setting forest fires, and so on. Furthermore, since examples given of things only men do are often all reprehensible, there is the suggestion that Aristotle identifies 'acting rationally' and 'acting rationally well.' But of course he is looking for the distinctive activity that, if performed well, will be constitutive of the good of man qua man. If there are difficulties with Aristotle's view, they are not those of such objections.

It will have been noticed that Aristotle no sooner introduces a criterion for distinctively human action, namely, that it exhibit a rational principle, than he insists on the ambiguity of the phrase 'rational activity.' Activity can be called rational or human either because it is the activity of reason itself or because it is an activity of some faculty other than reason that comes under the sway of reason. This suggests that, if reason is what will enable us to cluster all human actions, as strategy or architecture enable us to cluster subgroups of human action, 'rational' is a floating criterion. The way in which Aristotle first suggests that his criterion may be taken in several ways (activity that is essentially rational, viz., the act of reason itself, and activity that partakes of or is obedient to a rational principle) adumbrates the distinction between intellectual and moral virtues. The former are the 'well' or excellence of rational activity in the primary and essential sense, the latter the 'well' or excellence of rational activity in the secondary and derivative sense. Doing an action well is the excellence or virtue of the capacity that enables us to perform that action.

But the picture swiftly becomes more complicated. The rational faculty itself is subdivided into theoretical and practical uses of reason. Thus, while human action and rational activity are identified, we are faced with at least three great groupings: theoretical rational activity, practical rational activity, and the activities of faculties other than reason that come under the sway of reason and are thus rational by participation.

We can now address the third and final question of this section. In what sense is the ultimate end one? At the beginning of the seventh chapter of Book One of the *Nicomachean Ethics,* Aristotle says this: "Therefore, if there is an end for all that we do, this will be the good achievable by action, and, if there is more than one, these will be the goods achievable by action." At the end of the same chapter, he writes, "Human good turns out to be an activity of soul in accordance with virtue, and, if there is more than one virtue, in accordance with the best and most complete." Does this not suggest that the ultimate end or happiness, since it is not one particular good among others, is constituted by the whole set of human actions done well, a set of virtues pertaining to rational activity in its various senses? When we look back from this vantage point at the objections raised against the concept of ultimate end, we see that it is mistaken to assume that Aristotle holds that there is some single activity to whose end the ends of all other human activities should be subordinated. He is not saying that some particular kind of action must become our dominant passion, as writing was for Henry James and politics was for FDR. Nor could he have committed the simple fallacy of the third objection. He is not saying that there is some one end, the same one, of all particular actions. Virtuous activity or living humanly well do not signify one thing because there are *different* kinds of rational activity and thus different kinds of virtue, and our happiness or perfection or ultimate end is constituted, not by some one virtue, but, to the degree this is possible, by them all.

But is this a completely faithful portrayal of Aristotle's thought? If happiness turns out to be the name of a set of virtuous activities, is it not nonetheless the case that for Aristotle this is an ordered set? 'Rational activity' is no doubt various in its great kinds, but the phrase would appear to be, not equivocal, but an instance of something said in many ways but with reference to one. Theoretical reasoning, whose end or good is the perfection of the faculty of reason itself, namely, truth, seems to claim priority. Furthermore, *theoria* or contemplation is spoken of by Aristotle as the preeminent good for man. But then it seems that contemplation, like writing novels for Henry James, is indicated as a desirable dominant passion for all men.

Well, much depends on how this is understood. It cannot

mean that contemplation could be the exclusive concern of any man. For Aristotle, this activity is necessarily episodic. Nor, since anyone's life must include more than contemplation, could the ends of other kinds of rational activity be 'for' contemplation in the sense that they are not first ends of and for themselves. It is difficult to know what could be meant by sacrificing moral virtues to the dominant passion of contemplation. For one thing, intellectual virtues presuppose the moral virtues, which is one reason Aristotle discusses the latter first.

The set of virtuous activities that constitute human happiness can be ordered in several ways. From the point of view of necessity, of temporal priority (and this is an abiding, not an evanescent, priority), the moral virtues and the virtues of the practical intellect take precedence over those of theoretical intellect. Of the task of metaphysics, Aristotle says that all other human activities are prior to and more necessary than it but that none is better. This is a way of saying that contemplation could never be an exclusive or dominant passion of anyone. So, we are left with the view that man's ultimate end is not some particular good among others but is constituted by a plurality of virtuous activities. That set of activities may be seen as ordered in terms either of necessity or of nobility. From the point of view of nobility, the senses of rational activity are graded in such a way that the virtue of theoretical intellect that is exercised in contemplation is highest and best. But there is always a *set* of virtuous activities constitutive of human happiness.

"Let this serve as an outline of the good." Aristotle's discussion of the human good, while it may not be vulnerable to the objections we have mentioned, nonetheless requires a good deal of development. Subsequent chapters will to some degree provide that development. Now let us see how St. Thomas expands on the concept of ultimate end as he found it in Aristotle.

THOMAS AQUINAS

The notions of ultimate end and happiness are treated at the outset of the moral part of the *Summa theologiae*. This treatment owes much to Aristotle, but there is a special crispness and clarity in Thomas's presentation of what he derives from the great pagan philosopher. There are as well addenda that we would expect from a Christian reflecting on the overriding point of human life. One of the puzzling things about the concept of ultimate end is that it seems at one and the same time an assumption about what all men actually do seek and something about which we should become clear in order to seek it. Confronted by the bewildering variety of human actions with their equally bewildering variety of ends in view, mindful of the seemingly endless diversity in the ways men organize their lives, we can find it odd to be told that somehow they are all up to the same thing. Moreover, the sought-for clarity concerning the ultimate end may seem to be a device that would call men to a uniformity of life. The claim about a latent sameness in the variety of actions and styles of life seems whimsical, and the prospect of homogeneous sameness should clarity about the ultimate end be gained is repugnant. The concept of an ultimate end of human action must both accommodate the fact that the vast majority of men do not seem to be aware of what it is and suggest how the creative variety in the ways men live is fostered rather than stifled when clarity about the ultimate end is had.

St. Thomas's approach to the notion of ultimate end is through the meaning of 'good,' what he calls the *ratio boni,* the character of goodness. The formal note under which one chooses whatever he chooses, or pursues whatever he pursues, is goodness. But the good is what is perfective, fulfilling, satisfying.

> It should be said that it is necessary that a man seek whatever he seeks under the formality of goodness *(sub ratione boni).* If it is not sought as the perfect good which is the ultimate end it must be sought as tending to the perfect good since something inchoative is ordered to its consummation. (*ST* IaIIae, q. 16, c)

This passage suggests a distinction between the particular thing or kind of thing that is sought and the reason for seeking it. If I want a glass of Guinness, it is because, as the advertisements say, I regard it as good for me. It slakes my thirst. It relaxes me. It looses my tongue for Hibernian repartee. Only a miserable sot would equate the object of this particular choice with goodness itself. Of course, there are miserable sots, those whose god is their belly, as St. Paul says. A glass of beer can in certain circumstances really count as an instance of what is fulfilling of me, but it does not exhaust the formality under which choices are made. When I decide to leave the bar and go home, I do that too under the formality of goodness. If there were some one end of action that exhausted the formality of goodness, that itself completely satisfied and perfected my desire, there would be an identification of the thing sought and the reason for seeking it, and I would be absolved of all need to desire anything else. It is because there is no action whose object is identical with goodness, which alone and completely perfects and fulfills the human agent, that there is always a gap between what I seek and my ultimate reason for seeking anything at all. The ultimate reason for seeking anything at all, the *ratio boni*, since it is shared by all human agents, permits Thomas to say that, as a factual matter, there is an ultimate end and all men pursue it.

> It should be said that we can speak of ultimate end in two ways, in one way according to the notion *(ratio)* of ultimate end, in another way with respect to that in which the ultimate end is found. With respect to the notion of ultimate end, all share in the desire for the ultimate end because all desire to achieve their perfection, which is the notion of ultimate end. But with respect to that in which this notion is found, not all men agree about the ultimate end, for some seek wealth as the consummate good, some pleasure, others something else. (*ST* IaIIae, q. 1, a. 6, c and q. 5, a. 8, c)

This passage indicates that ultimate end, in the formal sense of it, is not something that could enable us to discriminate between good human agents and bad. "Those who sin turn away from that in which the notion of ultimate end is truly found but not from the intention itself of the ultimate end, which they falsely seek in other things" (*ST* IaIIae, q. 1, a. 6 ad 1m).

We may find this notion reminiscent of G. E. Moore and moral philosophers like R. M. Hare who took their cue from Moore's observation that Good can never be equated with any of the things sought as good. This led Moore to speak of Good as a non-natural property quite logically distinct from the natural properties of the individual things men seek. Carrying this further, Hare treated 'good' as functioning in a purely formal way such that I am committed to a series of logical moves if I am morally serious in saying, for example, that it is morally good for me to renege on my debts. If I am prepared to generalize this and get rid of the personal pronoun and agree that all men may renege on their debts, even my debtors, then I am employing the term in a morally serious way. This series of formal moves says nothing about the action or kind of action that is being called good. Indeed, anything whatsoever can be called good so long as I am willing to make the requisite logical moves. Hare made this point with his famous example of the 'fanatic.' He imagines a man who wishes to kill Jews. If this example be generalized, he must agree that, should he himself turn out to be Jewish, he too is a candidate for extermination. Hare's 'fanatic' is willing to do that. This purely formal approach deprives Hare of any basis for saying that exterminating Jews is wrong in itself. That is why he must put quotes around 'fanatic.' There is no non-formal way in which a judgment on the exterminator of Jews can be made according to which he would be a fanatic and not merely a 'fanatic.'

The genesis of this surprising position lies in an undeniable truth. Moore was right to see that the equation of the end of a particular action or kind of action with goodness itself would lead to oddities, among them that if on one occasion I pursue Guinness as good and, on another, Pepto-Bismol, I would seem to have to say that Guinness and Pepto-Bismol are the same thing. To some degree what Moore is pointing to is a feature of general terms. I say that Socrates is a man and that Plato is a man, but I would not want to equate either individual with that in virtue of which he is a man, since then Plato and Socrates would be identical. From this we would not conclude that there is nothing about Socrates that leads me to call him a man and nothing about Plato that leads me to call him a man. But there is something else involved in the ascription of good to agents, actions, and their ends. Unlike 'man,' the term 'good' is in its interesting uses analogous, not univocal.

A cool drink in appropriate circumstances really satisfies a human desire; medicine in appropriate circumstances truly fulfills a human need. Both are good, but they are not good in the same way. A common mistake in the interpretation of Aristotle's conception of the ultimate end is to think that, in the end, he wants to equate the formality of goodness and the end of the activity of contemplation. But this could only be the case if contemplation completely assuaged human desire, if contemplation rendered all other needs and desires otiose. Clearly this is not the case. The activity of contemplation may be a constituent of the ultimate end, but it can scarcely be identical with goodness itself. Concerning speculative science, Thomas writes that "it is sought as a certain good of the thinker which is included in the complete and perfect good which is the ultimate end" (ST IaIIae, q. 1, a. 6 ad 2m). Thomas's formal notion of ultimate end, while it entails that no one kind of action aims at an end that completely and entirely perfects the human agent, is nonetheless realized in an ordered set of goods that are constituents of the ultimate end materially considered.

Human action is undertaken with an eye to some end that is sought as fulfilling or perfective of the agent. Given that whatever men do they do under the formality of goodness, Thomas can say that all men, simply by dint of acting, pursue the same ultimate end formally considered. The ends of particular actions, though always sought as perfective of the agent, sometimes are such that they truly perfect the agent and sometimes are such that they are falsely thought to perfect the agent. Thomas's way of introducing the concept of ultimate end provides him with a formal basis on which to say that all men are in agreement on it. He also accepts Aristotle's suggestion that 'happiness' may be taken as synonymous with 'ultimate end.' It is because he holds that the formal notion of ultimate end, while it cannot be exhausted by any particular goal or kind of goal, nonetheless is truly saved in a set of things perfective of us that, having identified the ultimate end as the *ratio boni,* he then goes on to examine a series of candidates for the role of happiness materially considered. In a way reminiscent of classical moral writers, he examines and dismisses wealth, honor, fame, bodily goods, and pleasure as the ultimate aim of human action, that is, as things that could exhaust the conception of that which is perfective or completive of the human agent. A distinctive note is struck when he argues that no created good can be man's ultimate end.

> For happiness is the perfect good which totally quiets appetite; otherwise, if there still remained something to be sought, it would not be the ultimate end. The object of will, the human appetite, is the universal good, just as the object of intellect is universal truth. From this it follows that nothing can quiet the will of man except the universal good, which is found in no creature but in God alone, since every creature has a participated goodness. Hence God alone can fulfill the will of man. (*ST* IaIIae, q. 2, a. 8, c)

God who is goodness itself is the only object that can exhaust the formality under which we desire and act. Perfect happiness for man thus resides in loving union with goodness itself, God.

One of the consequences of this is that Thomas must say that perfect happiness is impossible in this life. The reason for this goes back to the way in which the good for man is understood; it is the good achievable by the distinctively human operation or function. But it is rational activity that is distinctive of man. God may be the only object totally fulfilling of man's desire for the good, but He remains an object that must be achieved, so to say, by human action. The rational activity whereby God is achieved in this life is contemplation, an activity that is intermittent, episodic, discontinuous. At best, then, contemplation can provide us with but a fitful intimation of perfect happiness (*ST* IaIIae, q. 3, a. 2 ad 3m). Furthermore, to the degree that contemplation is a product of metaphysics, it involves an inadequate and somewhat murky conception of divinity (*ST* IaIIae, q. 3, a. 6, c). It is because we have only imperfect knowledge of God in this life that, even when we recognize that God is indeed the fulfillment of all our desires, we can nonetheless treat Him as one good among others and prefer lesser goods to Him.

As a Christian, Thomas sees man's ultimate destiny in loving union with God in the Beatific Vision, but that is a destiny realized not in this life but the next. This perspective enables Thomas to see the moral life as it was sketched by Aristotle with a new clarity. Whatever his convictions about the persistence in existence of the human soul after death, Aristotle is concerned in his moral writings with the good achievable by action in this life. Thomas, as a Christian, could not wholly share Aristotle's notion of the good life, but the Aristotelian conception provides him with the natural base on which to erect his account of the graced and supernatural life to which we are called on this side of Paradise as well as the other. In a later chapter we will discuss the impact of Christian faith on morality. Suffice it to say now that Thomas held that some such account as Aristotle had given captures basic naturally knowable truths about the nature of the good human life. Grace presupposes nature and does not destroy it.

Rational activity, which is the distinctively human activity, is not a univocal notion, which is why doing well involves a plurality of goods that are constituents of man's end. That which is perfective of human action is not some single good because rational activity is not a single kind of activity. The excellent or virtuous life involves a plurality of virtues. When we say that a term is used analogously, we mean that in a set of its occurrences we would not give for each occurrence the same account of what it means. A recurrent term that is susceptible of an identical account is said to be used univocally. Thus in

Socrates is a man
Xanthippe is a man
Frank Lloyd Wright is a man

a single account of 'man' can be given, perhaps 'rational animal.'
On the other hand, in the following list,

Pay your bill
Donald Duck has a bill
He's my Bill

we would give three distinct and unrelated accounts of the recurrent term. Finally, to take an example favored by St. Thomas, in

A man is healthy
A complexion is healthy
Jogging is healthy

we would give neither identical nor wholly unrelated accounts of the recurrent term 'healthy.' Thomas suggests that we would give a plurality of accounts that would be partly the same and partly different. In each account, we would mention health, but one account would speak of the subject of health, another of the sign of health, and the third of a cause of health. Furthermore, one of these accounts would take priority over the others, since complexion is the sign of health in one having it and jogging is the cause of health in one having it.

In somewhat the same way, Thomas sees a diversity in accounts of 'rational activity.'

Grasping first principles is rational activity.
Scientific demonstration is rational activity.
Contemplating the divine is rational activity.
Deciding what to do is rational activity.
Making a birdhouse is rational activity.

Sometimes rational activity has as its end the perfection of the rational faculty as such, the attainment of truth. Sometimes rational activity has as its aim the perfection of some activity other than thinking, an activity that can share in or come under the sway of thinking. We can see that there is gradation and derivation in these uses. We can also see why Aristotle and St. Thomas thought of the perfection of reason itself as the preeminent human good, preeminent but not exclusive. They were also aware that concern for the perfection of thinking is something of a luxury, possible only when rational activity of lesser kinds has achieved its end by introducing sufficient stability into society to permit some at least the opportunity to do geometry, say. It is because intellect is peculiar to man that the pursuit of its perfection in truth is seen as the most distinctively human good, far more so than those rational activities that involve features we share with beings less than ourselves. Thus the goods that constitute the ultimate end can be ranked and ordered in a way that reflects this objective priority and posteriority. Contemplation, though it cannot be the exclusive activity of any human, is objectively the best activity in which a human can engage. A man who so orders his life that whatever else he does is ultimately at the service of contemplation can be said to be leading the objectively best human life.

Needless to say, human society would be impossible if everyone did this. Furthermore, as we shall see, if contemplation is a virtue, it is so only in a secondary sense. The human condition requires that a person engage in such activity when he should, as he should, where he should, and so forth, and theoretical virtues do not as such ensure that a person will so act, any more than the virtue of art ensures that one will engage in artistic activity in a morally praiseworthy way. Those virtues that ensure the agent as such, and not merely the good of some aspect of his being, like thinking, or the good of some product of his activity, are comprehensive and pervasive in their direction of human life. Engaging in the pursuit of truth or in artistic activity are moral pursuits insofar as they are assessed not only in terms of the intrinsic criteria for their success but also with regard to that comprehensive good that is man's ultimate end. Here is the truth of the objection to ultimate end cited earlier which would have it that our good is the orchestration of many goods rather than the exclusive pursuit of one of them.

Some pages ago we asked if the conception of ultimate end must be taken to be a call to uniformity of life. It can now be seen how baseless that fear is. The moral ideal, whatever the objective ranking of its constituent goods, is open to an infinity of realizations. We need have no fear that the moral code is a cookie cutter.

3. Ultimate End and Moral Principles

Moral philosophy is a reflection on human action in an effort to make explicit its implications with an eye to articulating on a general level certain normative judgments. That is, moral philosophy is a kind of self-examination, conducted in relative tranquillity, aimed at enabling us to do well what we are already doing somehow or other. In this effort there will be talk of starting points and principles. Thus far we have been discussing the very first principle or starting point of human action, the ultimate end, recognition of which is embedded in any action that any human agent performs, at least with respect to its formal notion. This suggests that moral philosophy is a way of getting clear on what truly saves the formal notion of ultimate end and then articulating the means whereby it can be achieved.

There is, however, another model of moral decision than the end/means analysis, one that can be called the principle/application model. If the moral part of the *Summa theologiae* begins with a discussion of ultimate end as the first principle of moral consideration, one of the most famous or, for some, notorious sections of the work is concerned with natural law. In that treatment, we are presented with a number of highly general precepts whose application to our lives constitutes the moral task. In this chapter, I want to show that the end/means model and the principle/application or natural law model are compatible and indeed complementary.

The conception of moral philosophy given at the outset of this chapter suggests that moral principles are not discoveries of the philosopher so much as articulations of what is implicit in what is being talked about. This notion can be clarified by appeal to an imagined alternative to Thomas's assumption about the nature of moral philosophy. Talk of human action, of what men ought to do or what it would be good for them to do, could begin by imagining a group of inert people waiting in the wings for the outcome of the discussion. In the wings things simply are what they are; it is a world of facts and otherwise featureless. Pop, who may be assigned the premoral task of handling stagedoor johnnies, is frozen in fact with the rest. The problem of ethics is seen as getting those people on stage. How can we persuade them to become actors? How can we move them from Is to Ought, from the pale cast of thought to the vivacious verve of behavior? Perhaps a better question is: Why should the philosopher assign himself this impossible task?

St. Thomas, as had Aristotle, came reflectively upon himself and others already on stage, acting, doing, deciding, being good and bad. Sometimes this reflection involves talk on the part of the agents; more often it does not. Of course, reflection on action is expressible and is expressed in words, in the *Nicomachean Ethics,* in the *Summa theologiae,* in novels, columns, exhortations, and so on. This is the background for the claim that whatever we do we do for some purpose. The aim of action is the good. Action, purpose, desire, end, good. The great principle or starting point is the good, the formality under which we desire whatever we desire. The good is the desirable.

Now, as G. E. Moore pointed out, there are two ways of taking a term like 'desirable.' We can understand it as we do 'visible,' and then, as the visible is what can be seen, so the desirable is what can be desired. On this understanding of the term, the remark that the good is the desirable would mean that anything men can in fact desire is good. But we might understand 'desirable' as we do 'detestable,' and then, as the detestable is what ought to be detested, the desirable is what ought to be desired. In the first understanding of it, 'desirable' would be called a descriptive term, in the second an evaluative one. This brings us to one of the most pointless controversies of modern moral philosophy, a controversy bequeathed to it by Hume. How can we move from the descriptive to the normative, from fact to value, from Is to Ought? How can we get our actors on stage? That this problem did not arise for St. Thomas is a strength, not a weakness, of his moral theory.

What is desirable is so to someone, the desirer, and under a given formality, namely, that it fulfills, completes, or perfects him. Given human actions—and they are given—there is purposive behavior that always implicitly involves the judgment that the course of action embarked upon is preferable to not having embarked upon it or to having embarked upon another course of action. Obviously this does not mean that we always act with serene conviction or that we may not consider what we are actually doing a *pis aller* or that we may not soon and often change our course. We desire to do what we are actually doing. Let us speak of desirable$_1$ to cover what we do in fact desire. Desirable$_1$ involves the judgment that what is desired is perfective of the desirer. On the face of it, there seems little sense in saying that one ought to desire what he in fact desires. Nonetheless, it is because what is desired, desirable$_1$, may involve a mistaken judgment, as when what is desired as perfective of the desirer is not in truth perfective of him, that it can make sense to say that one ought not to desire what he in fact desires. Conversely, we ought to desire what we desire in the sense that the object of our desire ought to deserve the formality under which it is desired, viz., perfective and fulfilling. Let us use desirable$_2$, to designate objects that truly save that formality, the *ratio boni*. To say that we ought to desire what is truly perfective of us is not to introduce something that is not already present in any given desire, some new motive, some factor coming from we know not where. Any action assumes that desirable$_1$ is desirable$_2$. If we learn that desirable$_1$ is not desirable$_2$, we already have a motive for desiring what truly is desirable, desirable$_2$. This does not mean that we will necessarily act on our corrected perception, of course; knowledge isn't virtue. Besides, no course of action exhausts the formality of goodness. What it does mean is that merely factual desire, such as is required for the Humean problem, does not exist. The supposedly troublesome transition from Is to Ought suggests that the formality of goodness, that which is perfective and fulfilling, is not already present in any desire.

It is useful to mention these matters now when our aim is to relate Thomas's discussion of ultimate end to his discussion of natural law precepts. In the *locus classicus* of Thomistic natural law, the famous Treatise on Law (*ST* IaIae, qq. 90–108), Thomas in Question 94, Article 2, makes a transition from "the good is that which all things seek" to "the good is to be done and pursued and evil avoided." This move is exactly the one we have been discussing with regard to the desirable, and it is no more mysterious. The link with previous discussions of ultimate end is clear. What is novel is the dubbing of "The good is to be done and pursued and evil avoided" as the first principle of practical reasoning. The concept of precept and principle here suggests a discursive move in the direction of kinds of action that either fall under or are excluded by the principle. In short, a species of syllogism, an argument, is implied. The theory of natural law is at least the claim that there are a number of non-gainsayable principles whose application to the circumstances of action is what is going on in moral decision.

PRACTICAL REASON

Before discussing moral principles in this sense, it will be well to locate them in a wider context. In the article from the Treatise on Law mentioned above, Thomas speaks of the account of the good and the precept founded upon it as principles of practical reason. The comparison is with the theoretical or speculative use of the mind. The latter is concerned with the perfection of thinking itself, with the acquisition of truth, while the former, the practical use of the mind, is concerned with the perfection of some activity other than thinking, that is, with the acquisition of truth about what is to be done or made. The last distinction is between *actio* and *factio*. It is often by appeal to making rather than doing that Thomas illustrates the nature of practical thinking. This is the case in a celebrated passage (*ST* Ia, q. 14, a. 16) where he suggests that there are degrees of practical thinking.

The article in question asks whether God's knowledge of creatures is theoretical or practical, but prior to dealing with that, St. Thomas reminds his reader of the meaning of the distinction and says that there are three criteria involved. Depending on how many of these criteria are saved by a given instance of it, there will be grades or levels of practical thinking. The proposed criteria are (a) the nature of the objects known; (b) the way the objects are known; and (c) the intent, purpose, or aim of the knower.

a. With respect to the *objects,* Thomas speaks of theoreticals *(speculabilia)* and operables *(operabilia)*. This second class comprises whatever we can do or make. If what we are thinking about does not come within the range of what humans can do or make, it is so far forth a theoretical object, e.g., a natural object, or God.

b. With respect to the *mode of knowing,* a house, for example, is an operable object according to the first criterion, but we can think about houses in several ways. Most of us know about houses in pretty much the same way we know about physical or natural objects. We describe or define them, classify them as this kind or that, see various logical relations between them and other artifacts. But there is another way to consider houses, a way not possible with natural objects: we can see them as the products of human effort and set out the steps necessary for constructing one. This way of knowing operable objects, call it the prescriptive or recipe mode, is a practical as opposed to a theoretical way of knowing them.

c. The *intent of the knower.* The term of practical knowing is making or doing, that of theoretical knowing the possession of truth *sans phrase*. If one knows an operable object in a practical way but has no intention of putting that knowledge to use, the knowledge is so far forth theoretical. If the knowledge is embodied in the activity of doing or making, however, it is fully practical knowledge.

We can schematize the degrees of practical knowing that emerge if we use O for the first criterion, M for the second and E for the third, with subscripts p and t for practical and theoretical.

1. $O_pM_tE_t$: Virtually practical knowledge.
2. $O_pM_pE_t$: Formally practical knowledge.
3. $O_pM_pE_p$: Completely practical knowledge.

Moral philosophy would seem to involve both virtually and formally practical knowledge. When we give an account of 'good,' when we define virtue, voluntary and involuntary, deliberation, and intention, we are engaged in virtually practical knowledge. Moral judgments, at whatever level of generality, would seem to be instances of formally practical knowledge. Completely practical knowledge, the knowledge incarnate in action, is presupposed by moral philosophy and is what it remotely aims to guide. Against this background, let us look at Thomas on natural law.

NATURAL LAW

Although Thomas Aquinas is rightly looked to as a major proponent of natural law—the view that there are true directives of human action, which arise from the very structure of human agency and which anyone can easily formulate for himself—it is oddly true that there is only one place in the vast body of his writings where he engages in an extended and formal discussion of law and its various kinds. Any student of Thomas will realize how unusual this is. Given the nature and occasions of his writing, Thomas was called upon to discuss the same issues again and again, so much so that appended to almost every article in the *Summa theologiae* is a list of parallel places to which one can repair for other discussions of the same topic. There are indeed a few such references to parallel places in the Treatise on Law, but most of them are due to the ingenuity of editors rather than to the fact that Thomas is taking up anew matters he has discussed elsewhere. Most notably, there is no discussion parallel to the article that is the focus of our present concern, Article 2 of Question 94.

The article asks: Is there only one precept of natural law or are there several? What is meant by natural law? At this point in the Treatise, we have in hand only the definition given in Question 91, Article 2: Natural law is the peculiarly human way of participating in the eternal law whereby God governs the universe. Every creature comes under the sway of God's governance, but "among the others, the rational creature comes under Providence in a more excellent way, insofar as he shares in that Providence, providing for himself and others." The rational creature directs himself to his appropriate end and activity. Such direction is expressed in precepts—propositions express, laws command—and the question arises: Is one precept sufficient to express how we should achieve our appropriate end?

Thomas begins by likening the precepts of natural law—his use of the plural relieves the suspense—to the first principles that guide theoretical discourse: both are *per se nota,* known through themselves, self-evident, not derived. A proposition is such when no middle term is required to explain the conjunction of predicate and subject. Rather, from the meaning of the terms, one sees immediately that the proposition is true or false. In the theoretical use of our mind, we can distinguish between apprehension and judgment, since we must first grasp the meanings of the constitutive terms of a proposition before we can form a meaningful proposition of them. We might think that the logical form alone would suffice. Thus, an axiom of the propositional calculus, $p \vee \sim p,$ provides a form that enables us to know of any proposition and its contradictory, whether or not we understand the meanings of the constituent terms, that only one is true and the other false. I will return to this.

Continuing for now, Thomas next says that being is something no one can fail to know: "Being is the first thing apprehended, an understanding of which is included in whatever else is apprehended." Whatever we know we know as a being, whatever else it is. On the apprehension of being is grounded the first indemonstrable principle: One cannot simultaneously affirm and deny the same thing. Why does Thomas express the first principle in terms of affirmation and denial, which seem to call our attention to the logical order? As it happens, we find in his writings at least three expressions of the very first principle: (1) It is impossible for a thing to be and not to be at the same time and in the same respect; (2) One cannot simultaneously affirm and deny the same thing; (3) A proposition cannot be simultaneously true and false. (3) is surely reminiscent of p v $\sim p$. For Thomas, (2) and (3) are parasitic on (1). This follows from his view that we first of all know and then secondarily and reflectively know the way we know. For him, the logical order is made up of second order talk, which entails that (2) and (3) are special cases of (1). Needless to say, this does not prevent p v $\sim p$ from playing the role mentioned above, but of course it could not play that role if we did not already know the meanings of some propositions and thus the way the world is.

Just as being is the first thing the mind grasps, so the good is the first thing grasped by mind in its practical function of directing some operation. An agent acts for an end that has the note of goodness. The first principle of practical reason is grounded in knowledge of the notion of goodness. What is the notion of goodness or the good? The good is that which all things seek. This is what 'good' is taken to mean, just as 'being' means that which exists. But something is sought insofar as it is completive or perfective of the seeker. Thus 'good' does not simply designate an object of pursuit; it gives the formality under which the object is sought or pursued: as completive, as perfective. The first principle of practical reasoning, analogous to the first principle of reasoning without qualification, is this: The good is to be done and pursued and evil avoided.

All other precepts of natural law are based on this one, such that all things to be done or avoided pertain to precepts of natural law which practical reason naturally apprehends to be human goods. (*ST* IaIIae, q. 94, a. 2)

Of this first principle of practical reasoning proposed by Thomas, Eric D'Arcy has written that it is a purely formal principle that tells us nothing about the facts; he calls it tautologous, analytic and necessary (Eric D'Arcy, *Conscience and Its Right to Freedom* [New York: Sheed and Ward, 1961], p. 52). He adds that it is self-evident in the strict sense: "If someone says, 'X is good,' it is nonsense to agree that it is, and to ask whether it is something that should be desired and pursued" (*ibid.*, p. 53). Finally, he calls it a "logical principle" (*ibid.*, p. 54). D'Arcy seems to leave everything on the level of what we have called desirable₁ and does not see that desirable₁ already grounds the ought involved in Thomas's gerundives or the imperative force of the principle, as he sometimes states it. His tautology comes down to 'good equals desirable.' We have seen that the implications of desire and finality enable us to distinguish desirable₁ and desirable₂ and to say that, if what is desired does not really save the formality of goodness, we should not pursue it and ought to pursue what does, desire already committing us to that. Is the first principle uninformative? Yes and no. Just as the first principle of all reasoning tells us something true of everything, so the first principle of practical reasoning ranges over all objects of pursuit. As general, neither principle is as informative as less general ones, but the less general ones are about things covered by the general ones. Surely D'Arcy does not want to say that these first principles are logical in the sense that they tell us about how we think about things. As we have seen, for Thomas, logical principles are unintelligible apart from principles that express the way things are or ought to be. D'Arcy is right in suggesting that we certainly need more fine-grained guidance than is contained in "Good is to be done and pursued and evil avoided." But more particular advice is precisely the particularization of the general; it does not exist in a totally different realm.

Germain Grisez rejects the view that natural law precepts are tautologies derived by mere conceptual analysis. Of the first principle he says that it is involved in the judgments of both virtuous and vicious men as well as backsliders. "It follows that practical judgments made in evil action nevertheless fall under the scope of the first principle . . . and the word 'good' in this principle must refer somehow to deceptive and inadequate human goods as well as to adequate and genuine ones" (Germain G. Grisez, "The First Principle of Practical Reason, in *Aquinas: A Collection of Critical Essays,* ed. A. Kenny [Garden City, N.Y.: Anchor Books, 1969], p. 368). We may take this to mean that whatever is done is done under the formality of the good, that is, with the thought that it is perfective and fulfilling of the agent. In that sense, mistaken judgments come under the scope of the principle. But of course the precept is urging us to pursue what truly saves the formality of the good, not sanctioning our mistaken judgments. That evil is to be avoided is part of the principle, of course, and that is how vicious actions come within its scope. What we need is knowledge of goods that truly save the formality of goodness and that ground more informative precepts.

All other directives and precepts of natural law will be particularizations of the first one. That is, there is a plurality of apprehensions each expressive of some constituent of man's complete end or good. Let us have Thomas's text before us,

> It is because good has the note of end and evil is its contrary that all those things to which man has a natural inclination reason naturally apprehends as goods and consequently as to be actively pursued and their contraries to be avoided as evils. The order of the precepts of natural law is based on the order of natural inclinations.
>
> a. For first there is in man an inclination according to the nature he shares with all substances, insofar as every substance seeks to conserve itself in existence according to its nature. Following on this inclination those things pertain to natural law which have to do with the conservation of human life and the avoidance of the opposite.
>
> b. Secondly, there is in man an inclination to more special things according to the nature he shares with other animals. Following on it

those things are said to be of natural law 'which nature teaches all animals,' such as the joining of husband and wife, the education of children and the like.

c. Thirdly, there is in man an inclination according to reason which is proper to him, as man has a natural inclination to know the truth about God and to live in society. Thus there pertains to natural law what looks to this inclination, for example, that he should not offend those with whom he must live, and other like things.

The good as end or completion is the object of inclination or appetite. Man is a complex whole comprising a number of inclinations, each of which has its appropriate good or end. By enumerating these inclinations and noting their hierarchy, Thomas finds the basis for articulating more particular precepts than the first, most comprehensive one.

What is meant by the order of natural inclinations? This: There are goods that man shares with all creatures, other goods that he shares with only some other creatures, and some that are peculiar to himself. If the human good is the good that is peculiar and proportionate to the human agent, it must be perfective of him as the kind of agent he is. But man is a rational agent. Therefore, the good or perfection of rational activity is man's end. Why then does Thomas mention the inclination to self-preservation, common to all creatures and thus to man, and the inclination to reproduce and raise offspring, common to all animals and thus to man? Was it not just such activities as bear on these goods that were set aside in the search for man's function?

The goods aimed at by these inclinations are part of the human good, but only insofar as they are humanized, that is, insofar as they are pursued, not just instinctively, but as the aim or goal of conscious action. As human the pursuit of these given goods must be rational, deliberate, responsible. Natural law is not simply the rational recognition of physical imperatives, nor is it a judgment of how we should act that ignores the given teleology of the physical. Natural law relates to inclinations other than reason, which have their own ends, by prescribing how we should humanly pursue those ends. For Thomas, natural law is a dictate of reason, not a physical law. It is by coming under the guidance of reason that goods that are not peculiar to man come to be constituents of the human good. Sex is a human good not just as such but insofar as it is engaged in consciously, purposively, and responsibly. That is how it becomes a human evil too. There is no way in which humans can engage in sexual activity other than deliberately, which is why the animal part of our nature is always a part, never autonomous.

As dictates of reason, natural law precepts are rational directives aiming at man's comprehensive good. The human good, man's ultimate end, is complex, but the unifying thread is the distinctive mark of the human, namely, reason. Law is the work of reason. A man does not simply have an instinct for self-preservation that must be pursued at all costs. He recognizes life as a good and devises ways and means of securing it in shifting circumstances. Since it is not the only good there is, it cannot take automatic precedence over all other constituents of the human good. Similarly, man does not simply have a sexual instinct. Recognizing his impulse to reproduce, he rationally directs this activity so that the pursuit of its end does not jeopardize the other goods that are constitutive of his perfection.

One familiar with the opening discussions of the moral part of the *Summa theologiae,* discussions concerned with the human good and ultimate end, will see that the several precepts of natural law are directives aiming at constituents of the human good or ultimate end. The first and most common precept states that we should pursue what is truly perfective of us and avoid its opposite. Other precepts are articulations of this one and direct us to constituents of the end. We should preserve life in a way appropriate to a rational agent. We should engage in sexual activity in a way appropriate to a rational agent. We should rationally pursue the good of reason itself and particularly truth about the most important things.

The natural law precepts other than the first do not express means whereby the good mentioned in the first precept can be attained, as if they were instrumental to it. Rather they express means in the sense of constituents of the ultimate end. St. Thomas sometimes uses the traditional four cardinal virtues to point to constituents of the human good. Wisdom, justice, temperance, and courage aim at goods that are major constituents of man's ultimate end. The rectitude of reason itself is had by wisdom; the institution into human affairs of right reason is the work of justice. Temperance and courage remove impediments to this rectitude in human affairs.

The precepts of natural law are general directives to the ultimate end, the most general one pointing to the human good in all its amplitude, other very general ones aiming at constituents of the human good. It is because recognition of the ultimate end is implicit in every human action that Thomas can hold that natural law is valid for all men and at all times.

A word on the way in which natural law is a claim that there are moral absolutes. Let us mean by an absolute moral principle a judgment or precept as to what it is good for us to do that always has force or a judgment as to what we must not do that admits of no exceptions. The discussion of man's ultimate end and the development of natural law precepts gives us a sense of the human moral ideal. It is this ideal that provides criteria for deciding when precepts are absolute and when they are not.

Consider first negative precepts. Thou shalt not murder. Thou shalt not steal. Thou shalt not covet thy neighbor's wife. Why not? Because such actions always and everywhere thwart the human ideal. There is no way that you can murder well, steal well, commit adultery well—except metaphorically. Any moral code is going to have a fair proportion of such negative absolutes. Of course, it would be a poor moral theory that came through only as negative. That is why we must always remind ourselves that the basis for proscribing certain kinds of action is that they are inimical to the ideal, to human good or perfection. Negatives presuppose positives. Be temperate. Be just. Be generous. Such positive precepts call us to the ideal, but they do not specify or necessitate particular ways of being temperate or just or generous. This absence of specificity may seem to be a defect, but it is rather the liberating aspect of the moral ideal. There is an infinity of ways to be generous. This seems to open the door to what may be called moral relativism, but that is a topic to which we shall return only after we have considered a fundamental alternative to the account just given, indeed to this whole book.

A CLEAR ALTERNATIVE TO THOMAS

The reader may well wonder what alternative to the foregoing could possibly suggest itself, but the compelling clarity of the current account should not obscure the fact that, for a good many contemporary philosophers, our account is arrant nonsense as well as culpable naivete. In the first place, we have been assuming that there is a nature that all those who are human share, such that certain things are true of any of them insofar as they are human. But, it will be said, the very concept of a nature is at once a begging of the question and runs afoul of a naturalistic view of how we got here. If human beings, along with all other species, just arose as a product of a slow process of natural selection, whatever nature we are thought to share is a product of chance. It has no purpose built into it that we might discover. The fact that doing moral philosophy in the Thomistic manner not only invokes teleology in the case of human nature but of nature as a whole will, for many, consign it to the dustbin of history.

Earlier in this chapter we alluded to supposed difficulties concerning Is and Ought. The shortest way of summing up the alternative view to the approach we have taken is this: The way things are gives us no clue as to what we ought to do. Some version of this slogan has been abroad since David Hume, who once wondered how it is that people, after a suite of statements in which they tell us that this *is such* and that *is so,* conclude that something *ought* to be done. How derive that Ought from an Is? Characteristically, Hume simply posed the question, but the suggestion of the passage is that we ought not make such transitions from Is to Ought. We are not told where that 'ought' comes from.

Subsequent discussions spell this out, however, and, for the century just ending, the most influential work in this regard is G. E. Moore's *Principia Ethica*. The book is in English and was published in 1903; in it Moore speaks of what ever since has been called the Naturalistic Fallacy. William Frankena suggested that it could just as well be called the Definist Fallacy, since it concerns the relationship between the things we call good and the goodness we say they have. Let us say that Rollo is good. Or, to begin with a less complicated case, I say: "The Yugo is a good car." It is easy to imagine a dispute breaking out over this astonishing remark. You want to know what on earth I can possibly mean by calling the Yugo a good car, and, warming to the task, I begin to mention mileage, transmission, price, and the like when suddenly a silence falls over the room. We turn and there in the doorway is G. E. Moore. We are told in memoirs such as those of John Maynard Keynes that Moore could disconcert anyone by the tone of voice with which he asked, "What do you *mean* by saying X?" Otherwise self-confident chaps disintegrated before this Olympian query, much as a quizzical look might cause you and me to check our zippers or wonder if there is food on our chin. Wittgenstein is said to have said that Moore was a good example of how far you can go in philosophy without any intelligence whatsoever. An unkind remark, but the career of the Naturalistic Fallacy has been more durable than Moore's reputation. What is the fallacy?

If, in explaining why a Yugo is good, I say that it is cheap to buy and cheap to run, I will be thought to be explaining the meaning of 'good' in this case. That is, "A Yugo is good" comes down to saying that "A Yugo is cheap to buy and cheap to run." But if 'good' = 'cheap to buy and cheap to run,' then the account can be substituted for the word defined and vice versa. But that means that "A Yugo is good because it is cheap to buy and cheap to run" is equivalent to "A Yugo is good because it is good." The suggestion is that the only way we can avoid having 'value judgments' turn into tautologies is to realize that the properties of the object called good can never account for calling that object good.

Things happen fast after this. We are told that there is a wholly contingent relation between the properties of the thing and our calling it good by citing those properties—they really don't explain our calling it good at all. If the properties of a thing do not account for our calling it good, then, in Moore's memorable phrase, "Anything whatsoever can be called good." There is nothing in the makeup of a thing that requires, or prevents, our calling it good. There is a gap between fact and value that cannot be closed by citing facts about the valued thing.

Alas, we know we are doing philosophy when we find ourselves in such a Wonderland as this. Professional philosophers seem to have a predilection for counter-intuitive theories, doubtless a residual effect of thinking that philosophy must begin with the systematic doubting if not repudiation of everything we thought we knew before. Wanting to distinguish between statements in which we describe and statements in which we prescribe, philosophers end by denying that there is any logical link between prescriptions and descriptions.

It was not until 1956 that there was an effective countering of this dogma; in that year Peter Geach published, in the journal *Analysis,* a little essay called "Good and Evil." Geach reminded his reader of the elementary grammatical distinction between attributive and predicative adjectives. In the case of a predicative adjective, for example, "He is a fat philosopher," we can break the insult down into "he is fat" and "he is a philosopher." Double jeopardy, as it were. But when I say that "He is a good philosopher" I would hesitate to make this into two claims, namely that he is good and that he is a philosopher. 'Good' is an attributive adjective; it sticks to the noun it modifies. Now while there may be a contingent relation between obesity and the pursuit of wisdom—some fat people are not philosophers and some philosophers are not fat—the only way we can figure out what is meant by calling someone a good philosopher is to go into what it is to be a philosopher. Thus, making use of Geach's reminder, we can say that Moore's elementary mistake was to confuse predicative and attributive adjectives. Of course, it is only right that the point be made linguistically, since the philosophical tradition in which both Moore and Geach stood characterized itself as having made the "linguistic turn." This was not the Bronx cheer so much as the Oxbridge hurrah.

Fifty-three years had intervened between Moore's egregious mistake and Geach's grammatical correction. During that time, Anglo-American analytic philosophers had been busy analyzing evaluative and prescriptive statements and proposing accounts of 'good' in such remarks as "It is good to see you" and "When she was good she was very very good" and the like. If such statements said nothing about reunions or the episodically commendable behavior of a little girl, philosophers sought to say what 'good' did express. 'Approval' was an obvious candidate. When I say that lemon pie is good, I am not citing another characteristic of lemon pie, to be added to citric tartness, meringue-sweetness, and lightness of crust. I am just saying, I *like* lemon pie. *De gustibus non est disputandum,* no doubt, but if pressed as to the basis for my liking I would doubtless give non-philosophical friends one of those characteristics of lemon pie. Strictly speaking, of course, none of its characteristics, nor all together, could serve as a logical reason for my liking it—if Moore is right.

Philosophers typically spoke of such 'moral terms' as 'good' and 'bad' as expressing the approval or disapproval of the speaker. And they would allow that sometimes it is possible to adjudicate between conflicting value judgments by drawing attention to an overlooked natural property of the thing evaluated. When I mention that you can put four Yugos in a two-car garage, my interlocutor's frown fades, and he too now says "The Yugo is a good car." Was he swayed by my citing that further property of the

Yugo? Only because he tends to approve cheap cars that take up
only half the space of real cars. But there could be a third party,
maybe Charles Stevenson, maybe G. E. Moore himself, who con-
tinues to disapprove of Yugos. Nothing we say can bring them
around, and nothing they say can elicit our disapproval of Yugos.
And the reason again is that approval and disapproval are only
contingently related to the properties of the thing being evaluated. Anything whatsoever can be called good—or bad.

Stevenson promoted the view that evaluative terms have emo-
tive meaning; that is, they express the feelings I happen to have
when confronted with a given object or state of affairs. You and
Moore witness a man who has been lurking in an unlit doorway
suddenly spring out, clobber a handicapped beggar, and make off
with his styrofoam cup of change. Moore is appalled. He is sure
the assailant cannot be English or in any case a Cambridge man.
You look up from your watch. "Ten seconds," you say. "Beauti-
ful!" In short, you approve and Moore disapproves of what you
have both seen. You may spend some time establishing that you
are indeed commenting on the same event but in the end it is
clear that it is of the same deed that he approves and you disapprove. Neither his approval nor your disapproval is grounded in
what you have both seen, required by it, so to say. Moore's feelings are his and yours are yours, equally unmoored in reality.

But they are moored, perhaps, in psychological reality. The
psychic pain he reports on is real; the satisfaction you take in a
job well done is real. It has been noted that this has the consequence that you and Moore are really not in disagreement at all.
You are agreed about what happened, of course, but his reporting
on his disapproval and your reporting on your approval of it is
not unlike his saying he has a headache and you saying that you
do not have a headache. Reports on different feelings do not
conflict when there are distinct feelers involved.

You will of course recognize this view of moral judgment: To
say of something that it is good or bad is not to state something
objective about the world, but simply to report on feelings you

happen to have toward certain events. But others have other feelings. How gauche it would be of you to seek to impose your feelings on others. Emotivism began as one philosophical account among many but, as Alasdair MacIntyre has suggested, everyone seems to be an emotivist now. Check letters to the editor or op-ed pieces in almost any newspaper. If the writer is taking umbrage at someone else's moral judgment, he will invoke the emotivist account and accuse the other of seeking to impose his subjective feelings or views on others. The fact that others have different feelings is sufficient to show the subjective nature of all feelings.

Of course we are gloriously inconsistent about this, and a fierce naturalism returns when cigarette smoking or deer hunting are at issue. Somehow these activities are taken to be different from marijuana smoking and infanticide and wrong just because of what they are. So maybe MacIntyre should have said that what we now have is not Universal Emotivism but Universal Inconsistency. We are emotivists or naturalists, depending.

It was Jean-Paul Sartre who provided a metaphysical or theological basis for the non-Naturalism of moral judgments, a deep reason why Is can never ground an Ought. An atheist like himself, Sartre observed, has to be thorough-going. If God is dead and out of the picture, with Him must go everything that assumes His existence. Sartre felt that those who thought God could be excised and the world and society would still look basically the same are simply shallow.

Consider what the theist, the believer, holds about human beings. They are creatures of God. Now creation is thought of on the model of the human artisan who, when he fashions something, does so with an eye to some purpose. A can opener is made to open cans, a corkscrew to open the wine. A can opener that does not open cans is a bad can opener; quality control dictates that it be discarded. A corkscrew that does not make the removal of corks easy is a bad corkscrew, and out it goes. They are what they are because the artisan made them to do something; that is their nature, and their nature is a basis for evaluating them. If man is an artifact of God's, man has a nature that provides a measure of his action. Acts that thwart his nature are bad, those that fulfill its potential are good. That is, there are criteria of good and bad action antecedent to this person's doing anything at all. He will be good if he fulfills the purpose his maker has embedded in him, and bad if he does not.

In a Godless world, there are no natures because there is no divine artisan. Consequently, there are no guidelines I must consult before acting. I am free to do whatever I want; mine is a total freedom, not a freedom measured by what I am, what I am designed for. Sartre spells out this alternative because it is his own view. Our initial sense that with the dropping of all antecedent restraints life would be a lark is soon dispelled by Sartre's gloomy description of what absolute freedom is like. We are without excuse. There is nothing to diminish our responsibility for what we do. We are condemned to be free.

One finds this in *Existentialism is a Humanism,* and it should be required reading for those who think they can slip back and forth between emotivism and naturalism. Dostoevski's Aloysha said anything would be permitted if God did not exist—he took this to be a refutation of the denial of God—and Sartre agrees with the consequence if not with the refutation. This ultimate question about human destiny can not be long avoided when we do moral philosophy. And there are increasing numbers of people who do not avoid it and take the Sartrean or Nietzschean route, drawing out the implications of our not having a nature or a destiny or any basis at all in the way things are for appraising them one way rather than another. There is a *chic* nihilism abroad, one that has crept into an incredible decision by the Supreme Court, the so-called Casey decision, in which a Catholic Justice was addressing a restraint upon abortion fostered by a Catholic governor of Pennsylvania. Justice Kennedy opined that each of us has the right to define the universe as he wishes, to determine the point and purpose of our reproductive system, to approve or disapprove abortion. Anything goes.

Any tendency we might have to think that airy philosophy has no impact on the price of cigars can be dissipated by considering the trajectory from the *Principia Ethica* to the Casey Decision. The Supreme Court has made Universal Emotivism the law of the land. Since it is obvious that no society can long endure on such a basis, it is of supreme importance that moral philosophy be done as it was done by Thomas Aquinas. This emphatically does not mean that we must all agree with Thomas's subjective opinions—that would be to adopt the view that is the clear alternative of his. The strength of Thomas's view is that it is not his—it is ours, and it is ours because it is true.

SOME CRITICAL REFLECTIONS

A view of practical reason that regards knowledge of the world and of human nature as irrelevant to it is clearly a view different from what we encounter in Aristotle and St. Thomas. The theory of practical reason developed by St. Thomas is a good deal more complicated than the Humean view. We have seen that Thomas provides not just one but three criteria for practical reasoning, suggesting that such reasoning is more or less practical to the extent that it satisfies more or fewer of these criteria. One of these criteria is the nature of the object—is it something that can be made or done by us?—and from this point of view a quite factual and descriptive statement about a house will count as minimally practical knowledge. This suggests restraint in speaking of the practical simply in terms of syntax. Some want to restrict practical discourse to gerundive precepts. But "Feed the hungry" and "The hungry ought to be fed" are scarcely unrelated in appropriate contexts.

In *The Abolition of Man*, C. S. Lewis drew attention to the way in which the split between fact and value had invaded schoolbooks. It has become the foundation of judicial decisions. Small wonder that there is an assumption that there can be no transition from Is to Ought, from fact to value, in the formulation of natural law precepts. Earlier we suggested that it is anachronistic to wish this alleged fallacy onto Thomas. Indeed, the dichotomies involved, once thought to be sharp and distinct, have come to be seen as doing duty for a number of contrasts that cannot be reduced to unity. Jacques Maritain, in *Neuf Lecons sur les notions premieres de la philosophie morale* (Paris, 1951), made the point that all intellectual activity is concerned with value, truth value, for instance. And indeed truth is one of the basic values, and not only in the propositional calculus. The concern not to infer value from fact, Ought from Is, is a symptom of false fastidiousness. Worse, it is to take at face value one of the most fundamental errors of modern moral thought.

RELATIVE MORAL PRINCIPLES

Earlier we mentioned that natural law precepts are absolute in the sense that they admit of no exceptions. Negative absolutes exclude once and for all certain kinds of action as destructive of the human good: affirmative absolutes command us to pursue abiding constituents of the human good. If the moral ideal, the ultimate end, dictates that certain kinds of action should never be performed and urges upon us actions that aim at the human good, principles expressive of such judgments scarcely exhaust what we would expect of moral philosophy. Indeed, when we give advice to another—and what else is moral philosophy but a species of practical advice?—we seldom think we are providing guidance that must necessarily be followed on pain of acting badly. St. Thomas puts it this way:

> That one should act rationally is right and true for all. Now an in- stance of this principle would be: Borrowed items ought to be re- turned. For the most part this is true, but it can happen in a given case that it would be hazardous, and therefore irrational, if borrowed items were to be returned. For example if the lender [say of firearms] is threatening the borrower's country. Now the more circumstantial such judgments become, e.g., were it to be said that borrowed items should be returned under such and such conditions, with caution, and in such and such a manner, the more defective they are: the more particular conditions enter into the statement of the judgment, the more ways the judgment can be defective and leave obscure whether or not one ought to make the return. (*ST* IaIIae, q. 94, a. 4)

This passage suggests three levels of moral Philosophy. First, there is the sketching of the ideal, of the ultimate end. The human agent being what he is, his good or perfection will be such and such. Since he is complex, his good will be complex, but there is a structure within those goods, and 'acting rationally' encompasses them all. Secondly, there are precepts that are absolute, and they are of two kinds, negative and affirmative. The affirmative precepts express ways and means without which the ideal cannot be achieved. The negative ones prohibit types of action that always and everywhere thwart the ideal, e.g., do not steal, do not lie, do not commit adultery. Thirdly, there are precepts, affirmative and negative, that enjoin or prohibit actions that by and large ensure the attainment of the ideal or by and large thwart it. But there are exceptions.

The example that Thomas gives, "Return borrowed items," expresses a way in which, by and large, justice will be served. 'Be just' admits of no exceptions, in the sense that we cannot imagine a fulfilled or good human being who is not just. But this particular way of honoring the good of another, by returning to him what we have borrowed, is not an absolute. By and large, it is a good rule to follow, and all things being equal, we should follow it, but it is easy *to* imagine circumstances in which it would be absurd to do so.

You have borrowed your neighbor's shotgun. When you return from the hunt, you are told by several people whose word you have no reason to doubt that the neighbor whose shotgun you have used to bag your quota of mallards has, in the interim, been announcing to the skies that at the first opportunity he means to blast you to kingdom come. Perhaps he has come upon piles of dead leaves at the end of his garden and is convinced that you have been pitching detritus over the fence and onto his property. To keep matters simple, let us say that this time he is wrong. You are as innocent as the driven snow, not to say fallen leaves. Very well. You arrive home, take off your boots, mix a toddy and are about to sink into the comfort of a chair, when the doorbell rings. You answer it. There on the porch with eyes aflame stands your neighbor. "I want my shotgun," he roars. Now, if there should flutter across your mind the thought that, after all, the shotgun is his, he lent it to me, and I should return it to him on demand, the thought will surely be followed by the realization that it is unwise to hand over to a man who has threatened your life the means to carry out the threat, no matter that the means are his property. Is this mere rationalization, a self-serving consideration?

Well, think about it. If in different circumstances you were to return the borrowed gun, it would be to serve the end of justice. Would that end be served if in these circumstances you returned the shotgun? Surely not. You would be aiding and abetting someone in the perpetration of an injustice—namely, blasting innocent you to kingdom come. It is an interesting thought that it is the same thing that justifies a principle like "Return borrowed items" and justifies exceptions to it.

Natural law precepts are absolute guides for human conduct that do not admit of exceptions. Other moral principles express ways of achieving the end or good envisaged by natural law precepts, and these principles can admit of exceptions.

If we think of moral rules or principles as stated in the form of universal affirmative or universal negative propositions, it would follow that any exception to the rule would be its falsification. Thus, if "Every act of lying is wrong" were conjoined with "Some act of lying is not wrong," we would have a contradiction, and one or the other of these propositions would have to be false. The same would follow if we conjoined "Sometimes justice should not be served" with "Justice should always be served." If a universal were thus falsified by a particular or singular proposition, we could reformulate it as "Most acts of lying are wrong." Some have been tempted by this altered form of the principle, because they want to argue that there are indeed occasions when lying is permitted. Some Calvinists hold a version of this idea and feel that it is a consequence of our sinful condition that sometimes we must do the wrong thing. We will see later how Thomas views the agent who is *perplexus*, that is, caught in a moral dilemma where, no matter what he does, he will be wrong. One who is in this condition, Thomas argues, is responsibly in it and is not therefore exonerated. In any case, Thomas insists on universal prohibitions, like that against lying.

We can retain the original principle "Every act of lying is wrong" and conjoin with it "Some acts of intentional deception are not wrong," and the result would not be a contradiction. The subjects of the two propositions are not the same, but of course there is similarity between them. An act that might have seemed to fall under the descriptive term 'lying' actually escapes it. Another example would be the compatibility of "Every murder is wrong" and "Taking a man's life in such-and-such circum stances is not wrong." That is, killing a man does not always amount to murder. Of course, this does not mean that there are exceptions to the universal prohibition of murder. Rather, there is a taking of human life that does not count as murder and thus does not come within the scope of the prohibition.

It has been objected that this comes down to saying that the wrongful taking of human life is wrong and that thus such principles are tautologous and unhelpful. Nothing could be further from the truth. The problem of action is to identify particular possible actions as actions of a given kind. If they are instances of a kind it is never permitted to do, this is extremely informative for the agent.

But we are touching on matters that form the topics of later discussions. We turn now to Thomas's analysis of the structure of human action.

4. The Structure of the Human Act

The activity that is peculiar to the human person is rational. This central claim does nothing to preclude the reality of spontaneous activity on the part of human persons. Neither, and more importantly, does it preclude habitual activity. We are unlikely to accept as the account of a human act the sort of explanation Conrad's Lord Jim gives of his leaving the ship: his feet jumped. Jumping involves the feet as tickling does the fingers, but such words are in a quite different category from those that designate muscular activity: spasms, twitches, and the like. The latter are not acts we are held accountable for because we do not think of them as emanating from reason and will. Human actions are voluntary actions.

In the present chapter, we will discuss (1) the notion of voluntary, involuntary, and non-voluntary action; and (2) the various component acts of reason and will that Thomas sees as making up a complete human action.

VOLUNTARY, INVOLUNTARY, NON-VOLUNTARY

Human actions are conscious willing actions, voluntary actions. Because they involve both knowledge and will, actions will be less than human or voluntary insofar as there is a defect in one or the other component. Violence diminishes or destroys the component of will and ignorance the component of knowledge.

Now, on the face of it, it seems impossible to say that an act of the will can be coerced or forced, since this would not be a kind of will-act but the negation of what we mean by willing or acting willingly. And, indeed, St. Thomas denies that the will can be coerced by an outside force. What sense are we to make, then, of the notion that violence can be done to the human agent, of the claim that, in some sense of the term 'act,' he can be forced to act?

If, when I am crossing the campus, someone pushes me and I go careening eastward, you would not, if you had noticed what had happened, ask me why I changed directions. *I* did not change directions. So too if a sudden gust of midwestern wind picked me up and bore me fifty yards to the south, I would not be said to have moved fifty yards in the same sense as when I direct myself fifty yards to the south. The latter is a voluntary action, the former is not. In the former case, I was forced to move, I was moved by force. But was my will forced? Can anyone force an act of my will?

St. Thomas makes a distinction between two senses of an act of the will, and it is relevant here. In a first sense, there is what he calls the elicited act of the will: to want or wish something. In such an act I use or exercise my will as such. In another sense, there are acts that are commanded by will and that involve the exercise of some capacity other than willing, acts like walking, speaking, raising my hand, and the like. Only acts of will in the second sense can admit of violence. If I sometimes willingly walk, I can sometimes be forced to walk. That is, the activity that usually follows upon my wanting to perform it is sometimes forced by an outside agency, another person, the wind, a sudden dipping of the deck on which I stroll. For Thomas, it is axiomatic, almost a matter of definition, that an elicited act of the will cannot be forced. No one can make me want something, force me to will. In order for that to be possible, the activity would have to proceed from me and not proceed from me at the same time.

The distinction may seem obscured in the following example. I am hurrying along the boardwalk toward the salt water taffy stand when my arm is suddenly grasped and I am propelled

through the swinging doors of a tavern. Against my will. I had
been going for taffy. As I am propelled across the sand strewn
floor, however, the aroma of beer assails me, my resistance ceases,
and I cooperate in my progress toward the bar. Is this a forced or
willing action? Thomas would say it is two actions. The first is
forced. My abrupt change of direction does not proceed from my
mind and will. Once my direction has been changed, however,
the tinkling piano, the seductive slide of sand beneath the soles,
the smell of beer alter my desire as well as my direction. As soon
as I assent to what was initially forced upon me, a new and voluntary act commences.

But perhaps another and more subtle form of violence is at
work now. I am helpless before the combination of honkytonk
piano and beer. The grasp on my arm no longer does violence to
me, but the properties of beer in such a setting overwhelm me.
Where the bee sucks, there suck I. This Bud's for me.

Like Aristotle, Thomas dismisses this objection. Violence implies an act contrary to what I do will or would will. The helpless
sot who slides willingly toward the bar is doing nothing that
conflicts with his desire.

Thus 'voluntary' like 'act of will' has two senses, and in one
sense of 'voluntary' we can be forced to perform acts which, when
commanded by the will, are voluntary. I may move my limbs and
use my other powers willingly, but coercion of them by an outside
force renders their activities involuntary, and then they escape the
moral order. We cannot be asked to give an account of why we
perform them because it is not we who explain their occurrence.
This comes down to saying that neither kind of voluntary act, as
voluntary, can be forced, but the difference remains that the elicited act of the will is such that it can never be coerced while acts
which when commanded by will are voluntary become involuntary when they are explained by an outside agency.

There are difficult cases, however. I am driving across the desert, my gas needle reads one-quarter full, which means I have
four gallons left, and my car gets twenty miles to the gallon. A

roadside sign tells me that the next service station is ninety-five miles ahead. The sun burns overhead. Sweat stands on my brow. I consider the heavy cargo of philosophy books stacked in the back seat and loaded in the trunk of the car. My calculation on mileage is based on the present weight of the car. It occurs to me that, if I get rid of the books, my mileage will increase and I may make it safely to the next service station. If I should run out of gas fifteen miles short of that station and have to continue on foot, I would run the risk of dying in the desert. Pondering these things on the side of the little-used road where I have parked to review my situation, I am assailed by fanciful velleities. The gas gauge is so made as to conceal the presence of one more gallon when the needle points to Empty. If I run out of gas, a friendly Samaritan will come along with a can of the requisite petrol and lend it to me. Would it be wise to rely on either of these happy eventualities? What if I am wrong? I bestir myself and begin to pitch philosophy books out of the car where they can waste their sweetness on the desert air.

A major assumption of this example is that it cuts me to the quick to unload philosophy books like this. Considered in the abstract, throwing away philosophy books is something against which I resolutely set my face. Yet now, in this plight, I throw them away and drive off with tears in my eyes. Do I act willingly when I thus scuttle my library? It is not something I want to do. If I throw the books out, it is because I fear death in the desert. Does not this fear, like coercion, render my act involuntary?

Thomas accepts the terminology that would call such deeds a mixture of voluntary and involuntary behavior. In such a case, I do what I do not want to do. But what does it mean to say that I do not want to get rid of my library? It means that as a general proposition it goes against my grain. But in the concrete circumstances in which I find myself, I want to get rid of the books because I want something else more, namely, survival. Taken as this particular deed in these circumstances, Thomas holds that getting rid of my beloved books is voluntary. What is done out of fear is, here and now, voluntary, even though that kind of action, prescinding from singular circumstances, is not one I would want to perform. That is why, in a manner of speaking, the singular act of discarding my books can be said to be involuntary, although strictly speaking it is voluntary. This comes down to saying that I take responsibility for throwing away my library in those circumstances. I would be a fool not to. That does not mean that I enjoy it. Those tears in my eyes are real.

It has occurred to many to say that concupiscent or sensual desire can make otherwise voluntary actions involuntary. Thomas will have none of this. Something is voluntary when the will seeks it. Sensuality inclines the will to want what is desired so sensuality renders an act voluntary rather than involuntary. This does not mean that it makes the action good, of course, only that we must answer for what we do under the inclination of sensual desire. The sequel to being taken by surprise by a pair of roguish eyes while walking through the park one day is voluntary, whether we practice custody of the eyes and continue on our way or, with dancing eyebrows, detour down the primrose path of dalliance. Now it is true that, as in the case of fear, the act so done may be the kind of act one deems evil. One may want to act temperately in the sense that one sees temperate action to be good. But in the singular case, here and now, drawn by the promise of sense pleasure, one wants what promises pleasure, and his general and prior wish is no longer operative.

This suggests an amendment to what we said of voluntary acts done out of fear. In the above example, the singular voluntary act of getting rid of the books is a good one. But this does not mean that fear always justifies what we voluntarily do when fearful. There are certain kinds of act that can never be performed well even when we fear the consequences of non-performance. Aristotle wisely said that we feel pity and pardon for those who perform demeaning acts out of fear. It is not as if they were acting in sunny and normal circumstances. Nonetheless, there are actions so heinous that we think one should die rather than perform them. If they are performed, we may feel pity still, but pardon may have to come from God.

Acts that when commanded by will are voluntary become involuntary when they are explained by force or coercion. The defect here is on the side of the willing component of action. But willing implies awareness or knowledge, and lack of knowledge, ignorance, can also render an action involuntary. Thomas's discussion of the role of ignorance in human action is nuanced.

He begins quite straightforwardly by saying that ignorance can cause involuntary action because it is the privation of the knowledge that is presupposed by the voluntary. But not just any ignorance can play this role. There are three ways, he suggests, that ignorance can be related to the act of the will: concomitantly, consequently, and antecedently.

Imagine someone acting who does not realize what it is he is doing. Oedipus marries a widow without knowing she is his mother. He does not see what he is really doing, and, if he did, he would recoil in horror from the deed. Or consider another case. I want to slay my neighbor. I am out hunting. I spot a deer which then disappears, and I go in hot pursuit. Movement ahead suggests the deer is there, and I shoot. When I reach the spot, I find that I have killed my hated neighbor and not a deer. But that is something I wanted to do. This second example is one of antecedent ignorance, the first an example of concomitant ignorance. The adverbs and adjectives are not important. The point in both cases is that the agent acts in ignorance of what he is really doing. The signal difference is that, in the one case, what I have really done is something I would have done willingly had I known. This is an example of what Thomas calls non-voluntary action. When what I really do is something I would not have done if I had known, the action is involuntary.

This contrast between involuntary and non-voluntary can be related to an earlier discussion. Involuntary action can be linked with bad luck, to which we attribute accidental effects of what we are voluntarily doing that go contrary to our will. Non-voluntary

action can be linked with good luck to which we attribute accidental effects of our voluntary acts that we would have brought
about had we known, Thus, involuntary and non-voluntary actions of this kind ride piggyback on voluntary action. I have to
be doing something, or intending to do something, in order to
be open to this kind of involuntary and non-voluntary action.

In some cases ignorance itself is willed and thus is voluntary.
Someone may choose not to inquire too closely into the circumstances of his actions because he wants to sin. Call this affected
ignorance. I do not want to know if the gun is loaded. I choose
not to ask whose money lies unguarded on the table. Sometimes
the will not to know bears not on the particulars of action but on
general precepts, as one might studiously avoid knowledge of
the laws that should govern his acts. Of course he will be held
accountable for this because his ignorance is voluntary.

It is of the essence of human actions that they be freely performed; my actions are within my power to perform or not to
perform; it is in my power that this action as opposed to that is
done. We pointed out in the opening chapter that it is useful to
distinguish between human actions and human life broadly taken,
the latter comprising all sorts of occurrences other than voluntary
actions. Nonetheless, Thomas's view of human action and our
freedom concerning it may seem unreal and abstract. He would
certainly be open to such a charge if he were taken to mean that
we are free to do anything or even anything possible for a human
agent to do. Each of us is limited in seemingly unlimited ways.
We have the talents and capacities we have and these differ enormously from person to person. Furthermore, during those years
before we can meaningfully be said to be capable of voluntary
action in Thomas's sense, we are trained one way or another, and
it is clearly possible for the bough to be bent in lots of unfortunate
ways. And we live in the society we happen to live in, one which
may institutionalize all kinds of evils. It is not simply that man
was born free and now is everywhere in chains. He does not

choose many of his circumstances; he does not choose to be born; nor does he choose all the accidents of birth and upbringing.

We may flatter ourselves that we are far more aware nowadays of such constraints on our freedom than Thomas was, and these constraints may seem of such importance that his apparently untroubled talk of voluntary action will strike us as having little to do with the human situation. Of course it would be too much to say that Thomas was unaware of the importance of upbringing or of the structure of the polity in which men live. For him, as for Aristotle, ethics is ultimately part of political philosophy, and it falls to the latter to discuss moral education. But whether the constraints on our ability to perform voluntary actions are discussed summarily or at length, their recognition leads to a large question. Is it possible for a human child so to be raised that it is unlikely in the extreme that he will be able to want or even to recognize the good? Are there circumstances that make human life, a moral life, impossible? Could evil be our good even without the defiant choice of Milton's Satan?

Part of the answer to this question lies in a person's ability to assess and appraise the moral education he has received. That appraisal and assessment can be of help only if true criteria are available to everyone. One of the functions of natural law in Thomas's view of the moral life is that it ensures that any human person, no matter what his moral education, will know at least the most general principles of the natural law. Indeed, the particular rules embedded in his moral education will be embodiments, however specious, of those general principles. Thus, entailed by anyone's actual moral education will be the principles according to which it can be assessed. But will such an assessment take place, and if it does, will it be acted on?

A full discussion of Thomas's reply to that question must await our final chapter, but suffice it to say now that Thomas holds that, without the aid of grace, sinful man is unlikely to achieve his natural good in anything but an imperfect way. Thomas's religious beliefs are not put in escrow when the actual human situation is the issue, and as a Christian he knows that man is in a state of sin, original and actual. This does not mean simply that, apart from Christ's redemptive action, man cannot be saved. His ability to achieve his natural end is also affected, with respect to his knowledge of it and, far more, with respect to his appetitive orientation to it. Thomas distinguishes between moral philosophy and moral theology, but it would be a travesty to portray his position as holding that everything is hunky-dory naturally and man's supernatural vocation is added on to a well-ordered moral life, personal and social. Grace builds on nature, but without grace nature's ability to attain its end is severely impaired.

For all that, human freedom, properly understood, is simply an assumption of Thomas's moral philosophy. The denial of freedom renders morality meaningless. Thomas will seek to clarify what is meant by freedom, but he never seeks to prove that man is free. Put most baldly, our freedom consists in the fact that none of the goods we seek can assuage our desire for unlimited goodness. Any course of action, any objective, has negative aspects and thus cannot compel the will. The only thing we will necessarily is our happiness, goodness itself, but in this life goodness is the aspect under which we pursue whatever we pursue and never a particular object or action. In this life, even God is a good among others and thus we can, tragically, sinfully, prefer created goods to Him.

There is another large question that must be at least touched on here. A dilemma for the believer, it would seem, arises from the fact that, on the one hand, he has no doubt that he acts freely and, on the other, he holds that every entity and event other than God, including human action, is a product of the divine causality. But does this not entail that what we call our free actions, since they are caused by God, cannot really be free and that freedom is an illusion?

The shortest form of Thomas's resolution of this difficulty is to say that God is indeed the first and ultimate cause of every entity and event but that He causes them in a way appropriate to their natures, which He has also created. Thus, because He has

created man free, He causes men freely to act, just as He causes
other effects to issue necessarily or for the most part from their
proximate created causes. What then if a human agent freely
chooses to act badly? Is God the cause of the evil? Thomas will
deny this consequence. The moral evil men do is ascribable to
them alone. Is there then something apart from God that He
does not cause? No. Moral evil is a privation, a lack of order. This
does not mean that we choose nothing when we act badly. Far
from it. We choose some good or what we take to be good. Sin
consists in choosing a good in such a way that it is not ordered
to other goods in an appropriate way. It is this lack of order that
is moral evil. These are little more than assertions, of course.
A full discussion of them would take us very far afield indeed.
Nonetheless, it has seemed well to say at least this much lest
Thomas seem to have overlooked a threat to human freedom his
faith might seem to pose.

ASPECTS OF WILLING

An act of the will, a voluntary act, is either an elicited act of the
will itself or the act of some other faculty or organ commanded by
the will. In his discussion of voluntary in the first sense, the various aspects of willing itself, Thomas becomes unexpectedly complicated. The will is the faculty whose object is the good. The
good, in Aristotle's lapidary phrase, is what all things seek, and
the distinctively human way of seeking the good is to desire the
good as known, as already cognitively present. We cannot want
what we do not know; the will is thus a rational appetite, a desire
that follows on cognitively grasping something as good. Something is grasped as good when it is related to us as something
perfective and fulfilling of us. The end, the objective of desire, is
good in the primary sense of the term. The means to the end is
also a good, but in a derivative sense.

When Thomas lays out the structure of the human act, the
complete human act, he distinguishes a number of different cognitive acts and different appetitive acts that follow on them. He

speaks of three acts of the will that bear on the end and three others that bear on means to the end. He makes the basic distinction because, while we cannot want what is for the sake of the end without at the same time wanting the end—the end is the reason for wanting the means—it is clearly possible to want an end prior to any consideration of the means necessary to attain it.

Also important for Thomas's analysis of the structure of the complete human act is the distinction between intention and execution. Prior to any overt act, there is a sequence of cognitive and appetitive acts that are the presupposition of overt behavior; elicited acts of will are presupposed by commanded acts of will. In recent discussions, a favorite example of a basic human act is raising one's hand. As something we do, this is not to be confused with someone else lifting our hand, or a nervous spasm that might cause our hand to fly up. Raising one's hand is a possible object of the question: why are you doing that? That is, the assumption is that I am doing this knowingly and willingly.

You are at an auction. Bids are mounting for a Ming vase that does not attract you; you are waiting for the batch of baseball cards that make up the next lot. Your nose itches, but you are wise enough not to scratch as bidders vie with one another for the vase. Finally, the sale is made and the next lot is introduced. The base bid makes your heart sink. It is already more than you meant to spend, but you raise your hand. Such a context is needed in order for the act of raising one's hand to work as an example of a simple human act. Given the context, it is clear that there is an inner prelude to the public lifting of your hand. It is the enactment of a deed you first think of and imagine; the enactment is voluntary in the second of the two senses we distinguished above. It involves the act of capacities other than just willing, in this case the motor capacity to lift your arm. What takes place prior to this commanded act of will is what Thomas means by the order of intention; the overt act, what we have called the enactment, is the order of execution.

In the order of intention, knowledge specifies the elicited act of will. It is this willing rather than that because of the object that informs it. Wanting vanilla ice cream differs from wanting a Roger Maris baseball card because of what we have in mind, the object proposed as desirable to the will. We are familiar with this emphasis on the primacy of the end. The end, which is the last thing in the order of execution or achievement, is the starting point of practical discourse, that is, it is first in the order of intention. As rational appetite, will follows on knowledge. Its first response to something grasped as good is to want it, to desire it. In English, as in Latin, we use the name of the capacity for its most fundamental act—will. Furthermore, the acts of will, since they follow on reason, are analogous to the acts of reason. Mind expresses itself in affirmation and denial; the will pursues the good affirmed and flees what is seen as evil.

But Thomas also speaks of reciprocal causality between mind and appetite. Knowledge of the good specifies the act of will, and Thomas says that, in the order of specification, mind moves will by presenting its object to it. This is formal, not efficient, causality. In the order of exercise, will is, so to speak, a self-starter. Its very nature is to tend to the good so that, when something is presented to it as good, all things being equal, it will respond by desiring it. The will can move our other capacities, including mind itself. I can choose to think. I deliberately put my mind to something. This reciprocity is sometimes summed up by saying that good is included within the object of intellect; it is a kind of truth that such-and-such is good for so-and-so. It is either true or false to think that something is good for a person, perfective of him. On the other hand, truth, the object of thinking, falls within the scope of the object of appetite: truth is a type of good. To know the truth is perfective of mind and of the rational creature.

The distinction between intellect and will does not blur because the way they act on one another differs. The mind is the specifying or formal cause of willing; the will is the efficient cause of thinking. It is a practical use of reason to think of things as good and thus to specify acts of the will (*ST* IaIIae, q. 9, a. 1 ad 2m). But the will as efficient cause moves the mind to think theoretically as well as practically.

A chicken-or-egg problem of priority seems to present itself here, and Thomas handles it by saying that the will just is the appetite for the good. That is its nature. That is what it is made for. Indeed, it cannot not will the good.

> [T]he will is moved in two ways: one with respect to the exercise of its act, another with respect to the specification of its act, which is from the object. In the first way the will is never moved necessarily by any object, for a person is capable of not thinking of whatever object and consequently of not actually wanting it. But with respect to the second way, the will is necessarily moved by some objects but not by others. (*ST* IaIIae, q. 10, a. 2)

Goodness itself, complete happiness, is the necessary object of will. Mind does not have the task of persuading or urging the will to be the will. Rather, in viewing something as good, it brings it within the range of the will's natural object. Does the will then necessarily desire that thing and the person go in pursuit of it? Obviously not. Nothing short of complete goodness or happiness necessitates the will. Doubtless it was because of this that Thomas saw the need to distinguish a series of will acts and acts of the mind as mediating between the apprehension of something as good and the active pursuit of it. The analogy Thomas uses is intellectual inquiry, which he thinks of as moving from principles to conclusions. In the practical order, the end is the principle or starting point, that for the sake of which all else is wanted.

> But will relates to the end in a threefold manner. In one way, absolutely, and thus it is called *will* [the act taking the name of the capacity], as for example we want health just as such, and other like things.* In another way, the end is considered as that which would

---

* The way Thomas speaks of health and other like things may be understood with reference to this: "The ultimate end necessarily moves the will, because it is the perfect good. Similarly those things which are so ordered to the ultimate end that it cannot be had without them, such as existence, life, and the like" (*ST* IaIIae, q. 10, a. 2, ad 3).

make desire cease, and in this fashion *enjoyment (fruitio)* looks to the end. In a third way, the end is considered as the term of that which is ordered to it, and it is thus that *intention* looks to the end. We are not said to intend health simply because we want it but because we want to achieve it through something else. (*ST* IaIIae, q. 12, a. 1 ad 4m)

When an object is seen under the formality of goodness, it addresses the will; the prospect of achieving it makes the will delight in it; and we can intend to reach it through appropriate means.

Intention motivates a person to deliberate concerning ways and means to achieve the end. The term of this process of inquiry makes choice possible. The process of anticipatory reasoning about action is the reverse of the enactment of the process. That is, presupposing the end and the will's relation to it, mind practically proceeds to seek means of achieving the end. When this process arrives at something that can be done here and now, the choice of that means leads on perhaps to intermediate means and ultimately to possession of the end sought. Thus, what was first in intention is the last in the line of execution or achievement. With respect to the will's relation to means, Thomas speaks of consent as well as choice. *Consent* is prior to choice because we can in deliberating about means find several ways to achieve an end, all of which are appealing. *Use* has to do not only with the employment of external objects as means but also with the will's relation to other powers that it sets in motion in our search for means to a desired end.

> The use of anything implies the application of that thing to some operation; hence it is that the operation to which we apply something is called its use, as riding is the use of a horse and striking the use of a stick. To operation however we apply not only interior principles of action, namely, the faculties of the soul or members of the body, e.g. the intellect to understanding and the eye to seeing, but also external things, e.g. the stick to striking. (*ST* IaIIae, q. 16, a. 1)

The will act that Thomas calls use will precede and follow choice depending on whether it bears on internal faculties or on bodily movements and external objects (*ST* IaIIae, q. 16, a. 4).

This quite complicated analysis of human action can be looked upon first of all as an indication of the way in which the particular choices we make are freighted with a presupposed structure. As rational actions, they are not episodic, mere blind moves. Implicit in them is an awareness of an appetition of some end-like good and the selection of means to its attainment through deliberation. Thomas's analysis also permits him to discuss these implied constituents of a complete action when they obtain, so to speak, discretely. There are wishes for objects that we take delight in and intend, prior to the search for the means of attaining them. A moral appraisal at this level is possible even if we go no further, since some things that we judge to be good, to fall under the formality of goodness, really do not, and this vitiates the will acts bearing on them just as it does subsequent acts of practical reason and will if we complete the action. Further, even when the end is truly good, we can go wrong in a number of ways with respect to our search for means. Not just any efficacious way of achieving an end is appropriate. As we shall see, it is a repeated maxim of Thomas that, in order for an action to be good, all its components must be good, but any defect makes it morally evil.

Thomas's distinction between the order of intention and the order of execution suggests that the sequence of acts of knowing and willing he has distinguished is a prelude to our doing something in another sense, precisely doing what we have been thinking of doing. Imagine that I recognize that a life of brain surgery would make a good profession for me; I dwell on it and take pleasure in the thought of myself probing among what Hercule Poirot calls the little grey cells; the intention forms in me to achieve this objective. How to go about it? Let us say that the thought occurs when I am a senior in high school. I deliberate about it, perhaps seek counsel from others, and a multiplicity of steps stretches out before my mind's eye. I consent to, find acceptable, several paths to the goal and then choose among them. At this point—and of course I may never reach it; the demands of medical school and the blandishments of Fifi LaRue, too impatient to wait for my patients and future revenue, may deflect me from my intention—the mind issues a command bearing on the ultimate step in deliberation, which is the first step in executing my plan. This could amount to writing a letter. The act commanded involves using my bodily organs and external objects: sitting down to my computer, hitting the keys, printing out the processed words. Other conceivable sequences could bring me to the commanded act of digging in the back yard, using the telephone, going to bed. These overt actions are arrived at via the complicated inner process Thomas has described. The commanded act, he will argue, is the same act as the command. That is, ultimately he wants the overt act to constitute a unity with the inner acts he has been discussing.

> So too in human acts, the act of a lower power is related as matter to the act of a higher power insofar as the lower power acts in virtue of the higher power's acting upon it, as the act of the principal mover is related formally to that of the instrument. Thus it is evident that command and the commanded act are one human act in the way that any whole is one though it has many parts. *(ST* IaIIae, q. 17, a. 4)

The foregoing has made clear that it would be wrong to think that Thomas means only bodily movements when he speaks of commanded acts. The act of will itself can be commanded, not in the sense that the will has to be commanded to want the good, but in the sense of wanting *this* good. So too an act of reason can be commanded in some cases and in a certain sense. Where the things we are thinking of are quite determinate, we must think of them as they are, as if forced by the nature of things, as Aristotle said. But, of course, we need not think of them at all. Thus, the specification of the act of thinking is not at issue, but its exercise. Of course, when we are thinking of matters that are indeterminate, we may command ourselves to think one way rather than another for reasons extraneous to truth, since determinate truth cannot be had. Here assent and dissent, as well as the exercise of thinking, are within our power and thus subject to command (*ST* IaIIae, q. 17, a. 6). Among the important objects of command are our emotions, our fears, and our desires, which can come under the sway of reason. Indeed, as we shall see, bringing our emotions under the sway of reason is precisely the aim of temperance and courage.

Thomas's procedure in analyzing action can raise a difficulty, since it may seem that, by starting from inner acts of mind and will, he is starting from what is more known than, say, the bodily movements involved in voluntary action. That is, we may wonder if Thomas holds that acts of mind and will are objects of introspection, direct and immediate objects of consideration. It is important to see that this could not possibly be his position.

Thomas's view of the trajectory of human knowledge is that only from knowledge of material things can we arrive at such knowledge of immaterial things as we achieve. But, for him, acts of volition and intellection are immaterial acts. Therefore, they can only be inferred. More specifically, he accepts from Aristotle the maxim that our powers and capacities can only be known from their acts. I know the will through an analysis of voluntary actions. Further, I know the inner only through the outer, so to say. Thomas's vocabulary in speaking of mental activity is instructive. It clearly involves the extension of terms first used to talk of material objects and events to the mental order. But we name things in the order that we know them. A moment's reflection on Thomas's account of intellection—as the reception of a form by the mind—shows that he speaks of coming to know on an analogy with physical coming to be. These considerations should suffice to allay the fear that Thomas, when he moves from inner acts to outer acts in his analysis of human action, is following what he takes to be the order of discovery. To portray his thought as involving immediate and direct inspection of the will and its activities prior to their overt manifestation would be deeply misleading since it would be a denial of his settled and reiterated view that any knowledge we have of things immaterial is founded on and derived from our knowledge of the material.

5. Good and Evil Action

At the outset we noted that Thomas's view of human action might seem to render a moral appraisal of it otiose. If every human action aims at the good, it would seem that every human action is good. To aim at the good is a necessary but not a sufficient condition of an action's being good, but even here there is need to distinguish the real from the apparent good. The will just is the faculty of the good; goodness is its formal object as color is the object of sight. But just as we do not see color in general but some particular color, so too we only will goodness as embodied in a particular end. And the particular thing that is the end is seen or known as good before it can be willed. To see or know it as good is to judge that it is perfective or fulfilling of the kind of agent we are. But we can make mistakes, corrigible mistakes, in thinking that an end or course of action is indeed fulfilling and perfective of us.

In what Thomas calls the order of specification—the kinds of things we judge to be good—reason obviously plays the central role and must be the measure of human action as human. In order for our intention to be good, it must bear on an end that is really and not merely apparently good. Intention, as we have seen, gives rise to deliberation and ultimately to choice, and what we seek in deliberation and select by choice is an act of a particular kind that will enable us to achieve the intended end. Does the end justify the means? Not necessarily. Thomas holds that there are certain actions that are of themselves bad and that cannot be justified because they aim at a good end. So too he holds that an action that is good in kind is vitiated if it is done with an eye to a bad end.

It is to the discussion of such matters that we now turn, and the discussion should serve to make clearer why Thomas went to such lengths in his analysis of human action. An action can go wrong in many ways—because of the end intended, because of the kind of thing done to achieve the end, because of the circumstances in which the act is performed. On the other hand, in order for an action to be good, it must be good in all respects (*ST* IaIIae, q. 18, a. 4 ad 3m). There are, then, multiple criteria for the goodness and badness of action, and it is necessary to distinguish the goodness and badness of the interior acts from the goodness and badness of the exterior overt commanded action.

A first general distinction, reminiscent of some we made earlier, is that between a natural process in which humans engage, described in itself, as a natural process, and the same process described as rationally engaged in by human beings. Seymour's beard is growing, and Seymour is growing a beard. The former is something that just naturally happens and can be described as such. The latter is a matter of intention, which is why we can ask Seymour why he is growing a beard. If we ask him, on the other hand, why his beard is growing, we would be surprised if personal pronouns showed up in his answer. The human act of growing a beard may seem an innocuous decision, but it would take on moral weight if someone were engaged in disguising himself, boycotting razor blade manufacturers, or getting ready to play a dramatic role. (Perhaps you know F. Scott Fitzgerald's story about Pat Hobby and Orson Welles.) Taken generally, it would appear to be a morally indifferent action. Nonetheless, Thomas is of the opinion that in the concrete no singular act is truly morally indifferent. The reason is that the intention with which it is done, if not the circumstances surrounding it, will make it either good or bad. Nevertheless, we would imagine that such actions are more often than not sitting lightly on the moral scales.

That Seymour's beard is growing and that Seymour is growing a beard are not both human acts. The first occurs willy-nilly;

Seymour is not answerable for it. If it were attributed to him, it would be like digesting, aging, breathing, and the like. All these activities can be truly said of Seymour, but we would not include them among the things Seymour does. But, as the undoubted example of a human act, Seymour's growing a beard, makes clear, human acts can include and give moral weight to events that otherwise would simply occur, and their occurring well or badly would not be a moral appraisal. My digestion may be bad, but all things being equal I am not blamed for this any more than I get moral credit for my sparkling blue eyes. Thomas dubs this distinction that between acts of man and human acts. We should not think, as some apparently do, that acts of a man are human acts before they get a moral appraisal, human acts in a pre-moral condition, so to speak.

If we take our power to reproduce ourselves, we are confronted with a process of far greater intrinsic importance. Here, as in the beard growing, we can explain the process without any reference to the intention with which it is done. But there is a crucial difference. Our beard just grows whether we are aware of it or not, but it would be odd to think that we might engage in sexual intercourse, that this activity would take place and only then would the matter of its moral appraisal come up. Still, it is possible to describe the act of sexual intercourse in such a way that we do not have sufficient grounds for any moral appraisal of it. A man and a woman are making love. What do you think about that, morally speaking? The answer is that we would have to know a good deal more than we are being told. At the risk of seeming prurient, we would want to know if the man and woman were married. If the answer were yes, then we would be likely to say that there is no reason to disapprove of what they are doing. This is not to say that the deed as described demands moral approval. It is possible for a husband and wife to engage in sexual intercourse with one another in a way that would be morally defective. But this criterion is enough for us to condemn the act, if the lovers are not married.

An abstract or inadequate account of sexual intercourse makes a moral judgment not yet possible, but this is quite different from the case of a man's beard growing. This is not to say that we would not invoke criteria for the activity taking place well or badly. If a foetus is malformed and is aborted before reaching term, we would say that the process of gestation has not taken place as it ought to. That is not what nature intends. Given the point of the process, we can speak of its being good or bad, but this is not a moral appraisal. Now, to the process so described moral conditions relate as supervenient ones (*ST* IaIIae, q. 18, a. 7 ad lm). From the moral point of view, the same natural process can fall under two different moral types, e.g., a marital act and an act of adultery (*ST* IaIIae, q. 18, a. 5 ad 3m).

Clearly this does not mean that humans sometimes reproduce themselves amorally and sometimes morally, as if the process could take place without our putting our minds to it. The natural process, in short, is something of an abstract entity. Human reproduction is always a human act, a moral action, good or bad. Our reproductive powers are within our power; we can use them or not. Reproducing, in short, is an example of what Thomas calls a commanded act. As a human act, reproducing is conscious, and for the activity to be morally good it must be consonant with the fact that we are rational agents. To use our reproductive powers merely as a means to pleasure or in ways that effectively deny what they are is repugnant to reason, much as the use of our taste buds and digestive powers in such a way that what they are is denied would be repugnant—for example, were one to eat, regurgitate, eat some more, regurgitate again, and so on with Neronian abandon. Such a use is an abuse, and one would be wicked not to recognize this. Equally, the reproductive act is repugnant to reason when the person with whom one mates is the spouse of another or not one's own spouse, and the consent of the partner does not diminish the injustice being done in this case.

When Thomas discusses the type or kind of act an action is, as opposed to the circumstances in which it is done and the intention with which it is done, he is not thinking of, say, the reproductive process in abstraction from its being humanly or rationally engaged in. What he calls the object of the action, that which we choose to do, that which makes it the kind of action it is, is the natural process taken, not abstractly, but as related to reason as consonant or repugnant. He gives as examples using your own property and using the property of others. Nonetheless, when he speaks of the goodness or badness of an action, he first mentions its (non-moral) goodness or badness as a process, in abstraction from its supervenient moral properties.

> Thus it is that a fourfold goodness in human action can be recognized. One which is generic, insofar as it is an action, since just insofar as it is an action it has being and goodness. Another which is specific, which is drawn from the object consonant [with reason]. A third according to its circumstances, as certain accidents of it. The fourth with respect to the end, as its relation to the cause of goodness. (*ST* IaIIae, q. 18, a. 4, c)

St. Thomas's use of the phrase "object of the action" is an ambiguous one, and it is not always easy to see what distinction he wishes to draw between the object of the will and the object of the action. If the action is the kind or type of action it is because of its object, and this is distinguished from the characterization of the action drawn from the intention with which it is done, we seem to have a fairly clear distinction. Thus if someone were to take another's property, steal his car, say, in order to rob a bank, his act would seem to have two counts against it. If he stole in order to give to the poor, however, his action might seem to have only one count against it, but that, as we have noted, would suffice to vitiate it. That order can be reversed, as when someone gives to the poor in order to be praised. Yet, in all these cases, the question "What are you doing?" seems answerable either with reference to the means or to the end. "I am giving alms." "I am feeding the poor." "I am improving my image." If the object of the act is what I am doing, it may seem difficult to appreciate Thomas's distinction between the kind of act an act is and the purpose for which it is done. The difficulty increases when he tells us that the specification of an act is taken from the end for the sake of which it is done.

The following passage, while lengthy, seems worthy of quotation here.

> In the voluntary action there are two acts, namely, the interior act of the will and the exterior act, and both of these acts have their objects. The end is properly the object of the interior voluntary act, and that with which the exterior act is concerned is its object. Therefore, just as the exterior act takes its species from the object with which it is concerned, so the interior act of will takes its species from the end as its proper object. However, that which is taken from the side of the will relates formally to that taken from the exterior act, because will uses the members in action as instruments, nor do exterior actions have the note of morality except insofar as they are voluntary. Therefore, the species of the human act is formally considered taken from the end and materially considered taken from the object of the exterior action. (*ST* IaIIae, q. 19, a. 6, c)

This passage enables us to see that the exterior act embodies the intention; it is what we are doing in order to achieve a purpose. However, when Thomas says that the exterior act takes on the note of morality only insofar as it is voluntary, he does not mean that its morality is assessable only in terms of the end. The process of deliberation that we considered in the previous chapter indicates that there must be a rational appraisal of the action possibly to be undertaken with an eye to the end. But the possible act may be repugnant to or consonant with reason quite apart from its efficaciousness in attaining the end. That action, the object of choice, may be relatable to a variety of ends other than the one currently engaging our interest, and a variety of possible acts could be efficacious in attaining the end that does engage our interest.

If there are two senses of 'object of the act' in Thomas—the object of the interior act and the object of the exterior act—there are also two senses of the 'end of the act.' That which the mind proposes to the will as good, that which is to be done, that which responds to the question "What are you doing?" is the end or good sought. Thomas calls it the proximate end in order to distinguish it from the remote end, that is, the further purpose for the sake of which one does what he does. The proximate end is synonymous with the object of the action, and its goodness cannot, as we have seen, be reduced to its efficacity in attaining the remote end.

The object of intention is an end-like good that reason judges to be perfective or fulfilling of the kind of agent we are. The moral quality of intention is dependent on the rightness of the rational specification of its act. The object of choice is the commanded act rationally specified as a result of the process of deliberation. Choice will be morally good if it bears on a good means. What makes a means a good one? Is it merely that it is an action that will enable us to achieve our end? Is the end the sole source of the moral quality of the deed we do?

In the twelfth century, Peter Abelard, in his *Ethics*, or *Know Thyself*, maintained with almost perverse glee that morality consists in intention alone and that the things we do, the actions we perform, are, apart from our intention in performing them, morally neutral. Is feeding the hungry good or bad? That depends on why we are doing it. If we do it for the glory of God, then it is a good action, but if we do it out of vainglory, it is bad. The same action can be, from the point of view of diverse intentions, either good or bad. Abelard does not stop here. Given the moral neutrality of the things we do, doing them can add nothing to the moral good or evil of our intention. That is, if you have the intention, it does not matter whether you fulfill it or not by performing an external action.

Abelard's little book is a seedbed of confusion and sophistry, and I do not propose to subject it to a close analysis here. I mention it because, although Thomas never cites Abelard explicitly in discussing these matters, it seems sometimes clear that he had his predecessor in mind in developing his own position. Thomas recognizes that some acts are morally indifferent, giving as an example the act of picking up a stick. As a type or kind of act, there seems to be no way of calling such a deed morally good or bad. But a token of the type, a singular instance of it, will always be good or bad, either because of the circumstances (e.g., the bishop is standing on one end of the stick when I lift it and topple him into the pews) or because of the end for the sake of which it is done (e.g., I pick up the stick in order to defend Fifi LaRue against an assailant, or I pick it up in order to assail Fifi LaRue with it). Abelard would have us see here the model of any and every action. Of course, this model alone suffices to show the incoherence of Abelard's position. In order for the deed I do to have moral goodness, it must be performed with a good intention. My intention to defend Fifi LaRue, say, is good because I intend something good. This can only mean that defending the innocent must already be a good kind of thing to do in order for my intention to do it to be thereby good. On the other hand, assailing the innocent, beating Fifi severely about the head and shoulders, must be a bad thing to do and thus render my intention to do it bad. Something is not good because I intend it; rather my intention is good because what I intend is good. Abelard himself, oddly enough, speaks of things that ought not be done, but he does not seem to realize that this destroys the strange dualism he wishes to maintain between inner states and external actions. Again, it is not my intention that makes defending the innocent good, but the fact that it is, so to say, already a good kind of thing to do that makes my intending of it good. We know that it is the sort of thing we ought to do.

Thomas does not stop at the truth that we must judge a goal to be good in order for our intending it to be good. Not every action we perform in order to attain the end is as a kind of action morally indifferent. Some actions are in themselves good or bad kinds of action. There are types of action that reason judges to be just as such morally good or morally evil. We have seen that the description of a human act without reference to its being deliberate and voluntary is an abstraction. Procreating can be described in quite clinical terms, without mentioning whether the partners are husband and wife, just as orgasm can be described without mention of the fact that the partner, if any, is of the opposite sex. Does this entail that the external act is morally neutral? This would follow only if such processes took place unconsciously and indeliberately, under hypnosis perhaps or while asleep, for then we would not say that the persons involved are initiating the action.

Since procreating is something humans do, they must do it wittingly, put their minds to it, choose to do it, and this entails that they think the act to be a good one. In order for the kind of act procreating is to be good, it must be seen in the wider context of the rational direction of our lives, and then whether the partner is or is not our spouse, is or is not of the opposite sex, has an essential bearing on the kind of act it is. Quite apart from our intention in performing them, such actions are good or bad in kind. If they are bad, no intention of a good end can render them good. If the action is in itself a good kind of act, it can be, if performed with an evil intent, morally bad. Thomas's position can thus be seen to accord a force to intention quite the opposite of what Abelard had in mind. A bad intention suffices to render morally evil an action that considered in itself is good in kind. But then circumstances can have the same effect. The marital act performed in the middle of Main Street at high noon is repugnant to reason, morally evil. However, there are no circumstances that can make an action evil in kind a good one any more than a good intention can do so.

The Abelardian tendency seems quite widespread nowadays, with moral theologians often speaking of the external act as if it were on a par with the circulation of the blood, the beard's growing, the ears hearing, or a spasm of the limbs. There is at once a description of action in such a way that it is no longer human action—procreating *sans phrase*—and a dualism of the outer and inner that makes the things we do neutral events whose moral quality is wholly derived from an inner state of intending something beyond what is actually being done. In fact, the external action as a human action embodies choice and command. It is the completion and fulfillment of intention and choice and cannot be understood, save in abstraction, apart from them. The external action as voluntary is essentially either moral or immoral. If the notion of the voluntary is to be taken to term, the good intended must be embodied in choices and in the performances of actions. To speak of actions as neutral appendages to inner states radically misconstrues what an intention is and what a choice is. An intention bears on an end judged to be good, and a choice bears on a possible action reason judges to be good.

Intention does not bear on the idea of a good but on a good of which we have an idea. Choice does not bear on a judgment but on an action judged to be good. The action judged to be good is not merely a natural process or event with its intrinsic teleology but a human involvement in that process; the rational appraisal is of it as something I might do. What is accidental to the natural process is essential to the moral action, namely, its being consonant with reason as performed in some ways and repugnant to reason as performed in other ways. To consider moral qualities as accidental to the actions humans perform is to reduce them to the status of mere events emanating from powers less than reason, e.g., our reproductive powers. But in a human action, reproductive powers are used in a rational way, and for humans reproducing is always either a good or evil action. "And in this way from the goodness of the will the goodness of the exterior action is derived, and vice versa, as one is ordered to the other" (*ST* IaIIae, q. 20, a. 3 ad 3m). The intention to perform a good act makes the intention good, and the good intention through choice effects the good action. Willing what is seen to be a good possible act leads to actually bringing about that action. If the will were not specified by a good possible act, it could not bring it about in actuality. It is the same act that from being possible becomes actual, e.g., giving alms to the poor. The goodness that the action has from the kind of act it is and the circumstances in which it is performed is the end and term of willing.

Since the action is what we choose to perform, its performance or nonperformance can scarcely be considered irrelevant.

Hence the will is not perfect unless it is such that, given the opportunity, it acts. However, if opportunity is lacking, the will being perfect in the sense that it would act if it could, the defect of the perfection which is from the exterior act is simply speaking involuntary. The involuntary, as it merits neither punishment nor reward in doing good or evil, does not detract from punishment or reward if a man quite involuntarily fails to do good or evil. (ST IaIIae, q. 20, a. 4, c)

If I mean to strike Fifi LaRue with that stick and you stay my hand, it is quite involuntary that I do not clobber her, and I get no credit for failing to do so. So too if I intend to give a bicycle to a child who has none and, when I go to the garage, find that it has been stolen, my failure to follow through on my intention is involuntary, and I am no less generous for that. Far from being standard cases of voluntary action, these are manifestly aborted instances, something clear from the fact that they can be discussed only with reference to standard cases. That the voluntary action can sometimes be prevented from reaching its fulfillment or term is an invitation to much self-deception on our part, something captured in the phrase that the road to hell is paved with good intentions. An intention that does not issue in action is a truncated one because action is what we intend.

Do the consequences of the actions we perform affect their moral goodness or badness? It would seem an odd conception of action that considered the consequences of action morally irrelevant. This is so because consequences often form part of our intention in acting. The rule that guides Thomas here is what we would expect. "The event which follows does not make into a bad act one that was good nor into a good act one that was evil" (ST IaIIae, q. 20, a. 5, sed contra). If you give alms to a poor man who then misuses the money you gave him, that does not make you less generous or your generosity blameworthy. If I assault Fifi LaRue with a stick with the result that she bears up under it patiently and nobly, this does not excuse my action.

Obviously it makes a difference whether the consequence of

an action is foreseen or not. If I foresee that doing the right thing will have all sorts of bad consequences, this must affect my judgment as to whether or not it is good to do it under the obtaining circumstances. Does the reverse follow? Could the conviction that performing an action bad in kind would have wonderful consequences justify performing such an action, by that very fact alter its moral character? The answer can be sought in the different valences of negative and positive precepts.

Negative precepts prohibit bad actions, and affirmative precepts urge to good action. But wrong actions are in themselves evil and can never become good in any time or place or other circumstances. Thus it is said that negative precepts oblige always and everywhere. But actions good in kind ought not to be performed just anyhow or anywhere, but in the appropriate circumstances, since these affect the goodness of the action. A good act should be performed when, where, and as it should be (*ST* IIaIIae, q. 23, a. 2, c).

Thus, no consideration of putative good consequences that might flow from it can justify the doing of an action bad in kind, but the consideration of evil consequences that are likely to flow from performing an action good in kind would prompt one not to perform it now, since he is not obliged in that way by the affirmative precept enjoining such action. Needless to say, consequences that are not and could not be foreseen, since they are rare and unusual, even when they assume tragic proportions, do not affect the moral appraisal of the action. The fortuitous or chance effects of our actions may play a great part in the story of our lives broadly taken, as we mentioned earlier, but they do not enter into the account of our moral life save insofar as they provide circumstances in which we go on to act morally.

Among actions that are evil in kind, Thomas mentions theft, suicide, adultery, lying, and the killing of the innocent. Generally speaking, the criteria establishing the absolute prohibitions of such actions are constituents of the human good that are thwarted by such actions. We turn now to a feature of Thomas's view of good and evil action that is utterly essential to his concept of the moral life. Moral actions are not realistically discussed as isolated occurrences. St. Thomas sees human agents as acquiring or losing a moral character, the stable disposition to perform actions of a certain moral kind—as possessing virtues and vices.

6. Character and Decision

The considerations of the previous chapter enable us to understand why we should want to distinguish between a situation in which a human agent does what is objectively and in itself a good act but where we are dubious about its motivation; a situation in which a good action is done and for the right reason and we are surprised; and finally a situation in which the right deed is done for the right reason and, given the agent, we are not in the least surprised. Such matters are best seen autobiographically. I can imagine myself giving alms to the needy, an objectively good thing to do, and nonetheless recognize that my motivation or intention leaves everything to be desired. I may want my department to meet the goals of United Fund so we can all wear little buttons in our lapels and get special mention at the banquet. If I had performed the right deed for the right reason, my action would be right, praiseworthy and meritorious. But, in my heart of hearts, I know it was the public recognition that motivated me, and this motive saps my action of its moral goodness. The fact that I act out of vanity deprives what I did of its good moral quality.

On the other hand, I can imagine myself doing the right deed for the right reason and surprising myself thereby; I have acted out of character. Alas, I do not expect such actions of myself. By a kind of idealization and extrapolation, I might imagine myself having a stable disposition to do the right deed for the right reason, so much so that it would be surprising if I did not act that way. Thomas, guided by Aristotle, considers such habitual dispositions—virtues and vices—as the sources of the actions we perform. A human life is a history, and we dispose ourselves, by the acts we perform, to do similar deeds in the future. Such a stable disposition to act well or badly is what Thomas means, respectively, by virtue and vice.

There is, for better or worse, a predictability in our lives, a stability of choice, an ingrained disposition to act in one way rather than another. We are disposed, because of the actions we have already performed, to perform similar actions in the future. This is what is meant by habit: a disposition to perform acts of a certain kind. "A virtue is a quality of mind thanks to which we live rightly, which can never be used badly." This is, in part, Augustine's definition of virtue, and it is with it that Thomas begins his discussion of the subject in the *Summa theologiae*. Aristotle's definition is different: virtue is that which makes someone good and which renders his action good. Human agents tend to be of stable character, good or bad, possessing an inner disposition to perform in the future acts similar to those they have performed in the past. A coward is disposed to act in a certain way in circumstances that threaten; the brave man is disposed to act in the opposite way in the same circumstances. One is not thought cowardly or brave because of the way he acts the first time he is exposed to mortal danger. A character is formed from the pattern actions assume in similar circumstances. Repeated acts of a kind dispose us—they do not condition or necessitate us— to act in the same way.

Is this a controversial claim? Thomas nowhere indicates that he thinks so. He seems rather to begin with the fact and attempt to elucidate and clarify it. It is as if the burden of proof is on him who would deny it. Are there or are there not patterns of action in our lives? Are these patterns strengthened or weakened by individual deeds? Do we, when we dream of moral reform, imagine the weight of our personal history as an obstacle to making the future unlike the past? Do we not imagine that, if only we could do such and such, then do it again and again, it would eventually be easier to perform acts of that kind? Of course we do. It is by way of being a fact of human action, and it is a fact Thomas assumes.

The recognition of this fact affects enormously our conception of what it means to perform a particular action. If we were tempted to think that we act in an historical vacuum, our decision and choice uninfluenced by what we are as a result of our past actions, the deed a simple matter of rational appraisal and appetitive pursuit, we would quickly be disabused of our optimism. The problem of the moral life is far more one of moral change or conversion than it is of performing an isolated act as it ought to be done. The depressing side of this realization is that it is very complicated to act in conflict with our past moral history; the sunny side is that, if our moral history exhibits a conformity with right reason, it is almost as hard for us to do something foolish and wrong.

If habit, the settled disposition to act in one way rather than another, is a fact of the moral life, it is obviously of the greatest consequence to acquire habits of the appropriate kind, good habits, virtues. But are there not counterexamples to this claim about moral character? It would seem so.

In his autobiography, Bertrand Russell recounts an episode. One day he was out bicycling, he says, and suddenly it occurred to him that he no longer loved Alys, his wife of the time. Now, it is that "suddenly" that is of interest. It seems clear enough that such a realization could be sudden, but at the same time it seems right to say that what is being realized could not have come about suddenly, unless we wish to retain the Romantic myth that we fall in love like meteors hitting the earth and fall out of it as we sometimes fall out of bed. Even if there were truth to Romanticism, such thunderbolt alterations of who we are, what we are, the self that is ours, hardly seem paradigmatic of what it is like to come to a decision that is momentous for our lives.

It is an unsettling thought that decisions of an important kind, the kind we tend to concentrate on in doing ethics, are not simply a matter of assessing a situation in the light of principles and then deciding, but are in some mysterious way made before we make them. Does it not seem reasonable to assume that, when a man leaves his wife, or vice versa, the decision is the cumulative effect of a whole series of minor decisions, each of them, when taken singly, of little moment—what the moralist would call indifferent acts—which yet, in the aggregate, in unforeseen and also unintended combinations, constitute the person we are when the momentous decision is to be made? Our dreams, our fantasies, our unspoken way of seeing ourselves and others, the shifting furniture of imagination, all those innocent reveries—think of what Thomas said of enjoyment and consent—are, in the view of the moral life that emerges, important because they are elements of our vision of ourselves and others. That is, the moral life is a continuum, not episodic as if it were composed of discontinuous *puncta* or moments.

Too often when we take a course in ethics, we are given for analysis moral problems of an altogether too dramatic sort. You are marooned in a lifeboat with four others and a limited supply of food and fresh water. Days pass on the briny deep. Food runs low, and water is at a premium. When is it permissible to eat the First Mate? Or, the city is under siege, surrounded by barbarians, and inevitably the demand is made. Release the king's daughter to the savage pleasures of the barbarian chieftain, or the city will be razed. What to do? The problem with such problems is that they suggest that most of us have never yet confronted a moral problem and are unlikely to do so in the future. If the moral life is made up of problems such as these, the moral life at best—or worst—would look like a line disturbed at rare intervals by pips of magnitude. But what goes on in the interim, in the interval between moral problems of the dramatic sort?

The answer has to be: the moral life. To be a moral agent is to be engaged constantly, throughout one's waking moments, in the endless task of incarnating in one's various and variegated decisions the moral good. This task may rarely reach a level that would attract a novelist. The truism that we are what we do should cover all our doings, perhaps particularly those that do not seem to be doings at all. It is the self so constituted that enters into the situation where big decisions are made, and it is that self that makes them, that sees and interprets the situation through what it has become by dint of all its doings, significant and insignificant. *Qualis unusquisque est, talis finis ei videtur:* as a person is, so does the end seem to him.

A man suddenly realizes that he no longer loves his wife, but the transition from faithful loving spouse to potential divorce is scarcely sudden. In the halcyon early days of wedded life, the honeymoon and beyond, a man strives and succeeds to see his life with reference to his beloved. He squelches impulses to act in a way inimical to their union. He overlooks and forgives actions destructive of unity of affection and outlook. Two become one flesh, but more importantly, two autonomous human persons adopt a common outlook and aspiration. The goal they seek is to see the other, in the Horatian phrase, as *dimidium animae meae,* the other and complementary half of my soul. This is an achievement, of course, not something bestowed by the marriage ceremony or the sacrament. The achievement is seldom a matter of deeds of a dramatic sort. A whole congeries of actions that, taken singly or viewed by an outsider, are insignificant conspire to form an outlook, a shared outlook. The union of spouses is made up of such elements as reading the same books, attending the same Mass, quarreling and making up, conceiving children and raising them—a whole series of deeds that foster union or threaten it. One could go on. What then does it mean to say that suddenly a man realizes he no longer loves his wife? Is this like succumbing to a virus, getting a tan, a risk one runs when bicycling? One wonders who might be riding on the handlebars. Such things do not happen suddenly. A series of minor infidelities—perhaps scarcely approaching the status of velleities—imaginings, dreams of an elsewhere and otherwise brought on by disagreements of a more or less substantial sort, the encouragement of fantasy—

these underlie the process. The process is gradual; the realization may indeed be sudden. But it is the realization of what one has voluntarily and responsibly brought about. It is no easy thing to change one's character or basic orientation; on the other hand, considering the constituent deeds, nothing is easier. The way to learn to play the harp, Aristotle observed, is to play the harp. Human choices of various kinds are either reinforcements of the loving pledge of fidelity to one's spouse or the gradual and subtle sapping of that pledge.

If this is true, the lifeboat approach to the moral life is fundamentally misleading. It is as hard to lose a good moral character as it is to gain it—well, almost as hard. The moral life is the daily turning of actions that for the most part are indifferent in kind to the moral goal. The failure to do this, what may seem to be the wait for the real and dramatic test, may surprisingly be an antecedent concession to the destructive alternative. The sudden realization that one no longer loves one's wife is the recognition of a pattern of action that favored rupture rather than union and disposed one to the blandishments of alternatives.

Here is the fundamental and abiding importance of seeing the moral life as a matter of habitual dispositions, virtues and vices, rather than as episodic choices made in the light of pure reason with little or no attention paid to previous personal history. Nonetheless, there are surprises. From a religious point of view, there are conversions as dramatic as Paul's on the road to Damascus. But even there it may be necessary, as Cardinal Newman found it to be, to write an *Apologia pro Vita Sua,* in which dramatic moral and religious change is seen as the cumulative effect of a whole series of antecedents that converged on a surprising point.

Since human actions by definition proceed from reason and will and are either good or bad, in order to be good they must proceed from correct reason and from a will that is oriented to the good. The habits that guarantee correct knowledge of the good and steady appetitive orientation to it are virtues. There are, then, generally speaking, two seats or loci of virtue—reason and appetite. In short, there are intellectual virtues and there are moral virtues.

Since we use our mind in various ways, sometimes to ascertain the truth of a matter and sometimes to guide our actions—that is, sometimes theoretically and sometimes practically—the intellectual virtues are at some times perfections of speculative intellect and at others perfections of practical intellect. Thomas follows Aristotle in recognizing three virtues of speculative intellect—understanding, science, and wisdom—and two virtues of practical intellect—art and prudence.

Understanding is concerned with the first principles of all reasoning and bears on immediate judgments, axioms, such as that it is impossible for a thing to be and not to be at the same time and in the same respect, that the whole is greater than any of its parts, and the like. Such truths are said to be immediate because no middle term is required to see the connection between predicate and subject. Rather, as soon as one knows the meanings of the terms involved, he immediately sees the truth of the judgment. And, since there are some terms whose meanings no one can fail to know, there are some immediate truths that are universally known. Thomas will speak of a habit or virtue of such principles, and this is what, in the speculative order, he means by understanding *(intellectus)*. In the practical order, the habit of first principles is called synderesis, and it bears on the most common precepts of natural law.

Not all truths are immediately seen to be such; most have to be inferred and are thus mediate truths. Thomas speaks here against the background of the syllogism, whose conclusion is known to be true as the result of the conjunction of true premisses. For example, I know Socrates to be risible because of the conjunction of "Every rational animal is risible" and "Man is a rational animal." What links man and risibility is rational animal, and then, since Socrates is a man, I know Socrates is risible. The skill needed to arrive at such derived truths is the intellectual virtue of Science. The third virtue of the speculative intellect is Wisdom, which relates all other truths to God. Wisdom, we recall, reflecting on the etymology of 'philosophy,' is the classical *telos* of the whole intellectual effort. Although one does not have to acquire Understanding, the other virtues of the speculative intellect are obviously achievements.

The end of the speculative use of intellect is the perfection of thinking as such, namely, truth. When we use our mind practically, we seek a truth for the guidance of activities other than thinking, e.g., the true good that the will should seek, the good in actions that involve the emotions, the good in activities in which we relate to other people. Generally speaking, Thomas recognizes two virtues of practical intellect—art and prudence. Art is correct reasoning about things to be made and aims at the good of the artifact. Prudence is correct reasoning about things to be done and aims at the good of the agent as such, taken either singly (ethical prudence), as a member of a domestic community (economic prudence), or as a member of a polity (political prudence).

Virtues that have their seat in appetite are virtues in a stronger sense than are the intellectual virtues. If virtue is that which makes the one having it good and renders his operation good, the recurrence of the term 'good,' which is the object of appetite, indicates why virtues whose subject or seat is appetite are more properly so called. Thomas sometimes makes this point by saying that intellectual virtues give the capacity to act well whereas moral virtues ensure good use as well. This is why virtues that have their seat in appetite are called moral, taking the root term *mos* to suggest custom, what it is natural or quasi-natural for us to do. In short, they give us the readiness to act in a certain way and not simply the capacity to do so.

The two main virtues having their seat in sense appetite are temperance and courage. Our concupiscible appetite bears on pleasures and pains; we tend toward the former and withdraw from the latter. In his Treatise on the Passions (*ST* IaIIae, qq. 22–48), Thomas provides a rich phenomenology of the emotions, remarkable in its scope. What he calls the irascible appetite has to do with goods difficult of achievement and pains hard to avoid. The emotions are in a sense a world unto themselves, appetitive responses to the sensed and perceived world. Sense appetite becomes the seat of virtue insofar as our emotional life can come under the sway of reason. Given the emotions that we more or less spontaneously and pre-morally feel, there are appropriate and inappropriate responses to their objects. The assessment of the appropriate and inappropriate, the morally good and evil, is made by reason. The stable and settled readiness to make rational judgments bearing on emotions is what is meant by moral virtue. The temperate man has an achieved ingrained disposition to act rationally when feeling the tug of promised pleasure.

The virtue having to do with those actions whereby we enter into relations with other persons has its seat in the will and is called justice. The will does not need any virtue in order to be oriented to the good as such since it simply is the faculty of the good. The good is its natural object. When reason articulates the necessary components of the human good, it can, so to say, present them to will as what the will already really wants. "Moral matters do not derive their kinds from the ultimate end, but from proximate ends which, though they are infinite in number, are not infinite in kind" (*ST* IaIIae, q. 60, a. 1 ad 3m).

From this analysis, there emerges the classical conception of the four cardinal virtues: prudence (wisdom), temperance, courage and justice. Thomas's Treatise on the Virtues (*ST* IaIIae, qq. 55–67) deals with, among other things, the integral or constitutive parts of these virtues and their subjective parts, or subtypes. This is done fairly schematically in *ST* IaIIae; in IIaIIae, he enters into the detailed discussion of the virtues and their sub-types. I mention this to indicate how impossible it would be to summarize his discussions in a way that would not be so sweeping as to be useless.

We must however, say something about the significance of the doctrine of virtues for our conception of moral philosophy. Aristotle remarked that we do not become good by philosophizing, by taking the fifty-drachma course in ethics, for example, and Thomas wrote that moral philosophy is of little or no value (*Disputed Question on Virtues in General*, a. 6, ad 1). Were these simply slips of the pen, indicative of a bad day on the part of their authors, or do they point to a truth about ethics that it would be foolish to overlook? Certainly sometimes one gains the impression that moral philosophy is put forward as if it were meant to provide us with intellectual skills that will enable us to act well. In some sense this must be true, or ethics would simply be a theoretical enterprise whose end is achieved when it provides us with a theory of action and a moral psychology. But surely we undertake the study of ethics in the hope that it will be of some help in guiding our actions and, indeed, in our acting well. It is precisely from this point of view that Aristotle and Thomas recognize the inadequacy of ethics. Their cited remarks can best be understood by seeing the difference between moral philosophy and prudence.

ETHICS AND PRUDENCE

Both moral philosophy and prudence are uses of practical reason with an eye to guiding actions. The differences between them are many, but the most salient is this: One cannot have the virtue of prudence if he does not have the moral virtues, whereas this necessity does not obtain in the case of moral philosophy.

> The reason for this is that prudence is right reason about things to be done, not only in general, however, but also in particular, since actions are particular. Right reason needs principles from which to proceed, however, but with regard to particulars reason must proceed not only from universal principles but from particular ones as well. With respect to the universal principles governing things to be done, a man is rectified through the natural understanding of principles thanks to which he knows that no evil is to be done, and also through practical science. But this will not suffice for reasoning correctly about

particulars. Sometimes it happens that a universal principle of this kind, known through understanding or science, is corrupted in the particular because of some passion, in the way that, to the concupiscent person, the good he covets seems good even when it is contrary to the universal judgment of reason. Therefore, just as a man is disposed to be rightly related to universal principles through natural understanding or through the habit of science, so in order to be rightly disposed to particular things to be done, which are ends, he must be perfected by certain habits thanks to which it becomes as it were connatural to him to judge rightly concerning the end. And this is accomplished through moral virtue. (*ST* IaIIae, q. 58, a. 5, c)

This passage suggests that moral philosophy is located between the habit of first principles, synderesis, which bears on natural law precepts, on the one hand, and, on the other, those particular judgments embedded in actions. Like natural law, moral philosophy proceeds at the level of generality. General judgments about what ought to be done are sometimes, Thomas says, destroyed by passion. This does not mean that, if we could only overcome our passions in the sense of stifling or overriding them, we would act well. Only when sense appetite is not the subject of virtue do passions prevent the general principles from having effect. In order for the principle to guide, it must be applied to the particular, and for this moral virtue is not only an aid, it is a necessity. We see the situation in which we must act through the lens of what we are, and that means how we are appetitively disposed to the good. On the level of moral philosophy, the good is viewed as a kind of truth (*bonum ut* verum). But the known good is something to be desired, and so long as it is not desired, so long as it does not function as good *(bonum ut bonum)*, there is incompletion (*ST* IaIIae, q. 19, a. 3 ad 1m). In order to judge truly in the particular case, and to command, mind is dependent on the condition of the appetite (*ST* IaIIae, q. 57, a. 5 ad 3m).

Here is the location of what some have found to be one of the more puzzling concepts of Aristotle and Thomas, that of practical truth. On the level of generality, we make judgments about what it would be good for us to do, and we can formulate precepts on the basis of such judgments. There has been much talk of *universalizability* in recent ethics, but the real moral problem is *particularizability*, that is, the application of these principles in the fluctuating circumstances in which we find ourselves, tailoring them to the here and now. This is the realm of the judgments and commands of prudence. Thus arises the crucial question: If on the level of generality judgments are true because they correctly express the way things are or the way they ought to be done, what measures the truth of the practical judgment on the basis of which the singular command, "Do this," is issued? The judgment of prudence is true, not because it is in conformity with the way things are, but because it is in conformity with moral virtue. Only if we are habitually ordered to the good, to the ends of the particular moral virtues, are we free to see how in the here and now these ends can be achieved. If we act contrary to what, on the level of generality, we know we ought to do, our action can be explained by the disordered condition of our appetites. On the other hand, when we act well, in accord with principles, and succeed in applying those principles to the concrete, this is a positive benefit of well-ordered appetite.

If what we set out to do in undertaking the study of moral philosophy is to be brought to success, namely, to performing good actions, the virtues must play an essential role. The doctrine of virtues is thus the centerpiece of Thomas's view of the moral life. It is not just knowledge of virtue we seek, but the acquisition of virtue, and virtues are acquired, not by the study of moral philosophy, but by repeated acts of a given kind.

There are two axes in Thomas's view of morality. On the one hand, there is the level of generality: first, the most common principles of natural law, which should guide our actions, and then moral philosophy proper, the quest of ever-less-general guidance for our lives. On the other hand, there is the axis represented by Aristotle's remark that, in moral matters, the good man is the measure. This remark may be taken to refer to the peculiarities of applying moral principles and the dependence of the judgment of prudence on the possession of moral virtue. The difference between moral philosophy and prudence can thus be simply expressed: The former does not depend for its correctness on the possession of moral virtue, but the latter does.

It could be argued that there is not so much a neat break here as a kind of spectrum. Does it not seem obvious that, in discussing some moral issues at the level of generality, the kind of person we are inevitably intrudes? Controversies about chastity, and sexual morality generally, seldom seem not to be influenced by the way in which the interlocutors behave sexually. Of course, passion—notably the desire to triumph, vanity, etc.—can influence discussions of quite theoretical matters. One sometimes detects the presence of passion even in modal logicians when they argue with one another. But in moral matters, one's appetitive condition with respect to the things being talked about can exercise a more direct influence. If this is sometimes so on the level of generality, it is always so when we act. As a man is, so does the end seem to him.

7. Prudence and Conscience

We would expect a correlation between the components of a complete action and Thomas's list of virtues, and this is what we do find. Mind as presenter to will of the end to be sought has the habit of first principles of action, a virtue called synderesis by Thomas. This is the habitual knowledge of the common precepts of natural law. For Thomas, the discussion of ultimate end and the discussion of the most common precepts of action hang together; they are not rival analyses. Furthermore, in his analysis of action, Thomas introduced deliberation as the inquiry undertaken to find good possible means for attaining the end willed. His discussion of prudence makes it clear that this virtue of the practical intellect is required to make the assessments that take us from the end desired through possible means to choice and thence to command or precept. If there are three acts of practical intellect involved here—deliberation, judgment, and command—it is the last that is the most important since the practical use of the mind is meant to issue in action.

> It is clear that with respect to the things a man can do, the chief act is to command, the other acts being ordered to it. Thus to the virtue which enables us to command well, namely, prudence, as to the more important, are conjoined as secondary euboulia, which enables us to deliberate well, and synesis and gnome, which are parts of judging well. (ST IaIIae, q. 57, a. 6)

Thomas simply takes over the Greek terms from Aristotle.

This should indicate the way we find a fit between the analysis of human action, on the one hand, and the virtues that perfect action, on the other. So put, the observation is of course banal, but the point is that the proliferation of virtues, if it is anything more than the proliferation of components of a complete action, serves to modify and complete Thomas's theory of action. That proliferation of virtues in Thomas's treatise raises problems. After all, Thomas is intent on bringing together a great many authorities and traditions when he lays out his own doctrine, and we find Aristotle and St. John Damascene, for example, interwoven in the same passage. Such a synthesizing presents the problem of establishing equivalences between diverse vocabularies. The problem of the relation between prudence and conscience is an important case in point.

Put most baldly, the question is this: Are prudence and conscience different or are they simply two names for the same thing? Josef Pieper thinks they are the same.

> The living unity, incidentally, of synderesis and prudence is nothing less than the thing we commonly call 'conscience.' Prudence, or rather perfected practical reason that has developed into prudence, is distinct from 'synderesis' in that it applies to specific situations. We may, if we will, call it the 'situation conscience.' Just as the understanding of principles is necessary to specific knowledge, so natural conscience is the prerequisite and the soil for the concrete decisions of the 'situation conscience.'*

Pieper thus calls synderesis natural conscience and prudence situation conscience. The first way of speaking is unfortunate from the point of view of interpreting St. Thomas, but the second, the equation of conscience and prudence, is at least initially plausible. Of both conscience and prudence Thomas says that they apply common principles to the particular. Why not regard them as two names for the same thing? Certainly, when Thomas speaks about conscience, he says things remarkably similar to what he says about prudence.

'Conscience,' he says, has three meanings that must be distin-

---

* Josef Pieper. *The Four Cardinal Virtues* (Notre Dame: University of Notre Dame Press, 1961), p. 11.

guished before the activity that interests us can be discussed. The Latin does not have two words, as English does, for consciousness and conscience, and that is why a first meaning of *conscientia* is awareness of what we are doing, as in "conscious action or behavior." Conscience, in a moral sense, is subdistinguished to accommodate two activities ascribed to it. On the one hand, conscience is a judgment made before we act which prompts, directs and guides; on the other, conscience assesses what we have already done and gives rise to remorse or satisfaction. In either case, conscience is an assessment of a particular action in the light of general principles. Thomas is somewhat stingy with examples here, but he does give, effectively, this: Adultery is wrong; Fifi is married and not to me; to have sexual congress with Fifi would now be wrong for me (and her).

Conscience is said to be an act, not a habit; a fortiori it is not a virtue. If it is an act, however, it must be the act of some faculty and, Thomas feels, of some habit of some faculty. The faculty is mind and the habits are several: synderesis, wisdom, and knowledge. We know that synderesis is the habitual knowledge of the first principles of the moral order, that is, the habit of natural law. Conscience is taken to be preeminently the application of natural law principles to particular actions. Moreover, this application is said to be deliberative and judgmental (*On Truth* q. 17, a. 1). Thus far, then, the account of how conscience operates, particularly antecedent conscience, looks to be indistinguishable from the account of the steps through which prudence moves toward commanding a particular action. So it is not surprising that Pieper and others have concluded that prudence and conscience are simply two names for the same activity. Indeed, it has been suggested that, when we consider the writings of St. Thomas chronologically, we find that in the early writings he assigned a large place to discussions of conscience whereas in later writings conscience all but disappears from view. Might we not then conclude that, as his thought developed, particularly when it flowered in the *Summa theologiae,* Thomas recognized the redundancy of the two notions, let conscience go and emphasized prudence? I think not.

In the *Disputed Question on Truth,* an early work, we find an extensive discussion of conscience. In the course of it, comparisons are made between the procedure of conscience and what is called the procedure of free will *(liberum arbitrium).* Both are concerned with the particular act; both presuppose general truths about how we ought to behave. Both, that is, presuppose synderesis and natural law. How do they differ? The judgment of conscience, Thomas says, is purely cognitive, whereas the judgment of free choice is not. The judgment of free choice reveals our moral character in a way that the judgment of conscience does not. In the way we discussed in the previous chapter, choices reveal our character, the condition of our appetite. But the judgment of conscience reveals our cognitive ability to see that a given act is forbidden, commanded, or permitted.

> That is why the judgment of free will is sometimes perverted whereas that of conscience is not; for example, when someone examines what is imminently to be done and judges (as it were still speculatively with reference to principles) that this is evil, for instance, to have sexual relations with this woman, yet, when he sets out to act in the light of this, other factors from a variety of sources come into play, like the promised delight of sexual activity, from desire of which reason is blinded and its assessment set aside. Thus one errs in choice and not in conscience, though he acts contrary to conscience and is said to act with a bad conscience insofar as his deed does not conform with his knowledge. (*On Truth* q. 17, a. 1)

This passage puts us in mind of what is crucial to moral knowledge and particularly to practical wisdom or prudence. The person described in the passage is defective. He knows what he ought to do, and he does not do it. This deficiency is not merely appetitive, though it is certainly at least that. If we say that there is a cognitive deficiency here, we would want to locate it in the decision that is embodied in the deed, and that decision is *Carpe diem,* seize the day, or in this case, the lady. We are not likely to think that such an agent requires more general information about how he ought to act. If he has a cognitive deficiency, it is not at that level. Or is it?

Recall the procedure St. Thomas follows in doing moral philosophy. He begins with the assumption that we act for some purpose, with an end in view. He holds that the good has been rightly described as that which we seek; that is, end and good are initially identified. The aim of action may only be to perform that action well; it need not have some product beyond the performance of the action. We are led on to a description of the 'good for man' in a way with which we are now familiar. This procedure requires that we first relate cognitively to the human good; that is, we can arrive at knowledge of what it is, and if we are successful our knowledge is, of course, true. But what we are speaking of is the good, and to speak of the good, to relate to it cognitively, to know it under the guise of truth, is not yet to relate to the good as good. The good is the object of appetite; it is what we seek, pursue, aspire to. Even at the level of very general principles, if the goods that are enunciated are not my goods, if I am not effectively ordered to them as to the objects of my appetite, these principles are not in the full sense moral or practical principles.

The ends of the cardinal virtues are constituents of the human good, of the ultimate end. The moral ideal, if it is merely known, cannot function as a moral ideal. I need those acquired dispositions of appetite that are called temperance, courage, and justice in order to be related to the moral ideal, to the human good, as good, as moral. In order to acquire such dispositions of appetite, moral virtues, I need the virtue of the practical intellect Thomas calls prudence. As has often been pointed out, there is a virtuous circle here. The moral virtues presuppose prudence, prudence presupposes the moral virtues. At the least, this means that they are acquired simultaneously. As to their interaction, the following picture is urged upon us. The moral virtues ensure an appetitive ordination to particular ends constitutive of the ultimate end. Prudence or practical wisdom determines how the moral ideal can be realized here and now; that is, thanks to prudence, we deliberate, judge, and command as to the means of realizing the end. It is here that the notion of practical truth makes its appearance. The judgment of prudence as to the means of realizing the end is said to be true, not by conformity with the way things are, but by conformity with the presupposed ordination to the end by moral virtue. Only if my judgment that courage is good is complemented by my appetitive ordination to that good as good can my deliberation, judgment, and command as to how that constituent of the ultimate end is here and now to be realized be effective. It is on the assumption of this appetitive ordination to the good as good that Aristotle could say that the mind's judgment, prudence's judgment, as to how the good can here and now be realized is executed *euthus,* straightaway.

Many of the difficulties raised against the notion of the practical syllogism as it figures in the process of prudence disappear when one sees the force of the phrase "the good as good." If the major premise is considered to be merely cognitive, action is not going to be the conclusion of the reasoning process. But when the good expressed in the major premise is my good, there is already the disposition that, when the means of realizing the good are found, prompts the choice of those means.

St. Thomas contrasted the judgment of conscience and the judgment of free choice by saying that the former is purely cognitive and the latter is not. In order for conscience to function there is required only a cognitive ordination to the good. I know what it is. Thomas, in illustrating how the judgment of free choice can be perverted, in effect describes the incontinent or morally weak man. He knows what he ought to do, his conscience is all right, but his knowledge of the good is not complemented by an effective affective ordination to the good as good. That is why, in the crunch, in choosing, he goes wrong. His heart is elsewhere.

Conscience is the purely cognitive appraisal of the particular in the light of general principles which takes place before or after action, whereas the judgment and command involved in free choice are embedded in the action and reveal the character of the agent.

Conscience is clearly a very important moral factor. It stands for those judgments of what I ought to do here and now that, alas, may go against the grain of my character, as becomes clear when I make my choice. Or conscience is the retrospective appraisal of what I have done, bringing on either remorse or satisfaction. It has been likened to a voice within, the voice of God, but when we hear it we realize it is our own voice, expressing what, thanks to the intellectual light of our nature, we know is demanded of us now. Its judgment is not the final one. It may be embedded in the act we go on to perform, or the act we perform may embody a contrary judgment, in which case the remorse we subsequently feel refers back to the antecedent judgment of conscience.

The recognition of the ultimacy of conscience may seem to have a devastating effect on the claim that there is objectivity in morals. We often hear appeals made to conscience that sound very much as if their point were that each person sees things his own way and that is the end of it. If one person says that premarital sex is wrong and another says it is permitted, are we simply left with two views? Before discussing that, let it be said that each person is indeed left with his own view. If I know that extramarital sex is wrong, I am obliged to act in accord with this judgment. He who holds the opposite is not so obliged. Clearly, if conscience is the ultimate court of appeal in moral matters, it looks as if we are saying that both a moral precept and its opposite can oblige at the same time in respect to different agents.

The threat of relativism is increased when we imagine two people speaking of extramarital sex with one saying, "My conscience tells me it's all right," and the other replying, "Well, mine doesn't." If this is meant to stop all moral discussion, then clearly conscience and appeals to it would undermine moral objectivity. A kind of action is wrong for me but not for you and vice versa.

The imagined disagreement is of course about a common principle bearing on a kind of action, not its application here and now, which is the proper task of conscience. It is better then to imagine the disagreement as bearing on an exception to an agreed upon principle or rule. But in either case we might seem to come down to an impasse where one person sees it this way and another person sees it that way. Since such claims are actually made, it seems well to say something about the confusions involved in them.

Clearly extramarital sex is either wrong or it is not. The judgment that it is unreasonable, repugnant, for human beings to engage in sexual activity unless they accept the full implications of it, an acceptance that is called marriage, is either true or false. It would be an odd, not to say tyrannical, conception of moral precepts that portrayed them as the imposition on others of my judgments, as if they were mine in the sense of having their origin in some subjective quirk in my outlook on the world. On the other hand, to say that moral judgments apply only to the one making them—I think murder is wrong, but make up your own mind—is so fraught with logical problems that one hesitates to begin to enumerate them. Ethics would be mere autobiography.

It is pretty clear that we do not really accept the ultimacy of conscience in this way. That the rapist and the one raped have different views on the morality of rape does not much interest us when we consider the kind of deed it is. Some acts are bad because of the kind of act they are; some acts are good in kind; some are indifferent, neither good nor bad as kinds of act. But what if someone does not know that a kind of act is always wrong? Surely the only knowledge that can guide the moral agent is the knowledge he has. Surely it is possible for someone to think that what is bad is good and vice versa. Surely too if I think that a certain kind of act that is really good or indifferent is bad, then I must act in accord with what I think. This means that, while appeal to conscience cannot be taken to mean that a given kind of act is both good and bad, or good and indifferent, or indifferent and evil, taking on different moral coloration simply because of the numerical diversity of the agents involved, nonetheless every agent is obliged to follow the judgment he makes.

To this it could be objected that the result is the same as it would be if we simply began by relativizing all moral principles. In the end, after all, people will act according to their own lights. Indeed, they are obliged to, and we have to accept the moral diversity that results. But of course we could not accept it. If your neighbor claimed that his conscience gave him the right to take things from your garage without permission, you would not take that to be the end of the matter. If your spouse claimed that his conscience did not forbid adultery, you would be unlikely to take that as you would a remark about his headache, freckles, or baldness.

Each agent is obliged to follow his conscience, but this is not tantamount to saying that every agent has a well formed conscience. It is erroneous to believe that theft is permitted. It is wrong to hold that adultery is all right. One is obliged to act on his own judgment, but he is responsible for making the judgment he does. If it is erroneous, we will be interested in his changing it. Indeed, we often prevent people from acting on their real or alleged views when those views are erroneous. Professional thieves are not considered to have an interesting and defensible concept of private property. As Thomas puts it, an erroneous conscience may bind, but it does not excuse.

When he discusses this question, he recalls, as we would expect, what he has had to say about ignorance as depriving an act of its voluntary character. Not to know the true nature of what I am doing would seem to deprive my action of its voluntary character. It could, but not necessarily. Sometimes ignorance itself is willed, and then of course it is voluntary. Knowledge that I am obliged to acquire and do not makes my ignorance voluntary.

> Therefore if reason or conscience errs by error which is directly voluntary or due to negligence, because it is error concerning what one should know, this error of reason or conscience does not excuse, and

to will in accordance with reason or conscience which errs in this way is evil. However, if the error is such that the act is involuntary, stemming from ignorance of some circumstance which is not due to negligence, then an error of reason or conscience excuses and to will in accord with it is not evil. (*ST* IaIIae, q. 19, a. 6)

Thus, one who wrongly judges that adultery is permitted and acts in accord with this knowledge acts wrongly. He is held to know better, and if he does not he must answer for his ignorance.

Conscience and its role do not, then, threaten the objectivity of morals. Indeed, without a theory that some acts are of a kind always to be wrong there would be no way to distinguish between a good and a bad conscience. And if there were not, the incoherence of the Abelardian position would soon engulf us. If it were the case not only that every agent must follow his own conscience but also that every conscience is true and well-formed, moral discourse would become babble. My judgment that an action is good or bad would be nonsense because I could not say what it is I am thinking when I think it good or bad. If minimally I should say it is good or bad for me, then I am either right or wrong in saying so and this is scarcely a private matter through and through. If conscience obliges it does not automatically excuse.

This may seem to have as consequence that a human agent can find himself in a position where he cannot not do the wrong thing. The term Thomas uses for such a person is *perplexus*. He is in a moral dilemma, damned if he does and damned if he doesn't. Imagine someone with an erroneous conscience. He thinks what is good is bad or vice versa. Well then, if he does not act in accord with his conscience, he acts badly, and if he acts in accord with his conscience, he acts badly. Thus, necessarily he acts badly. But that deprives him of the basic option in moral matters, and we might wish to avoid that unfortunate consequence by saying that to act in conformity with a bad conscience is good.

In discussing this, Thomas says it is true that in moral matters one evil being given another seems to follow necessarily from it.

He imagines a person who acts out of vainglory, and then it looks as if whether he does what this intention demands or fails to do it he will act badly. But Thomas does not agree that that leaves him in every way *perplexus*. Why? Because it is possible for him to alter his intention.

> So too, given an error of reason or conscience which arises from an ignorance which does not excuse, moral evil necessarily follows on willing in accord with it. But such a man is not *perplexus*, because he can recede from error, since his ignorance is vincible and voluntary. (*ST* IaIIae, q. 19, a. 6 ad 3m)

Needless to say, here as elsewhere we should notice the different valences of negative and affirmative precepts. No singular act that violates the negative precept can possibly be good, though it is always possible that in a non-culpable way we are unaware that a given act does violate the precept. Thus, in Thomas's example, a man who mistakenly thinks the woman snuggling up to him in the dark is his wife does no wrong in making love to her, though what he does is wrong and, when the lights go on, he would recognize the fact. The application of affirmative precepts to singular circumstances has an all but infinite latitude, since acts in their singularity are infinite (*ST* IaIIae, q. 60, a. 1 ad 3m). Socrates said of his daimon that it did not tell him what to do, only what not to do. We may think that conscience is like that, but it has as well the role of judging when the circumstances in which we find ourselves are opportune for acting in accord with affirmative principles, and here variety is to be expected. That a man should love and honor his wife covers all husbands, but the infinity of ways in which uxorial affection can be expressed and deepened prevents any interesting predictions about it.

The moral order is protected on its borders by negative precepts, but in the interior positive precepts suggest the inexhaustible openness of the human good.

8. Religion and Morality

In seeking to lay before the reader the moral philosophy of St. Thomas Aquinas in its grand lines, we have relied almost exclusively on a theological work, the great *Summa theologiae*. The fact that we could do this tells us something about Thomas's understanding of the relation between philosophy and theology, but something that can only be appreciated when we understand how, for him, the two disciplines differ.

A feature of the current situation in philosophy is that philosophers experience difficulty in explaining precisely what it is they do. A reason for the embarrassment is that so much of the original terrain of philosophy has been taken over by disciplines of latter-day origin that it is possible to think the whole of philosophy will eventually metamorphose into science and the ranks of the unemployed will become swollen with erstwhile seekers after wisdom. It was a response to this seeming threat to suggest that philosophy has no subject matter of its own but is a second-order discipline whose task it is to reflect critically on what is going on in disciplines that do have a subject matter. Hence, perhaps, the proliferation of such activities as philosophy of science, philosophy of history, philosophy of art, and so on.

Whatever the present situation, Thomas Aquinas operated with a conception of philosophy that had come to him from the Greeks. Understood as the pursuit of wisdom, philosophy becomes an umbrella concept under which are gathered all disciplines that are necessary for or conducive to the acquisition of wisdom, and wisdom is taken to be such knowledge as men can attain of the divine. Classically understood, the ultimate aim of the philosophical quest is called not only wisdom but also theology. For Aristotle, what we would call natural sciences—and he was the originator of many of them—were essential elements of philosophical activity, not something distinguished from it. He held this view because he held that it is only through knowledge of the natural world that we can come to such knowledge as we do of things divine. Logic, natural sciences, mathematics, ethics and political philosophy, literary criticism, indeed all the liberal arts, were sought not only for their own sakes but as stepping stones to the culminating science of metaphysics. It could be said that, in its classical conception, philosophy included most of what is done in our universities. One can only imagine Aristotle's puzzlement, accordingly, if he were to come upon a department of philosophy distinguished from many other departments. How can philosophy be understood as a specialty? It would have boggled his mind. Thomas would have found our situation equally surprising.

Nonetheless, Thomas had a more restrictive view of the range of philosophy than Aristotle did. If philosophy in the classical mode found its term in a discipline called theology, Thomas did not therefore concede that every consideration of God is simply a philosophical one. Thus Thomas felt it necessary to distinguish two kinds of theology, that of the philosophers and that of Christians. We may think, he suggests, of two kinds of truths concerning God. First are those truths about God that can be arrived at by unaided natural reason and that are derived from truths about the world. One need only think Of the Five Ways of proving that God exists that Thomas set forth in order to get a picture of the procedure of this natural theology. Second, there are truths about God that have been made known to us by God Himself through revelation and that are undreamt of in philosophy. The Christian accepts as true that there are three persons in one divine nature, that Christ is both human and divine, that we are called to a destiny of loving union with God, and many other similar things.

Think of the articles of the Creed. The theology of the Christian consists in reflection on the truths that God in His mercy has revealed to us about Himself.

That there is a God, that there is no more than one God, that God is the cause of all else, is intelligent, simple, and good—these are truths about God that Thomas thinks men can come to know simply by using their natural abilities. He takes it that these are truths some pagans did come to know, and *ab esse ad posse valet illatio:* what has been done can be done. The Trinity and Incarnation, on the other hand, are held to be true only because God has revealed them, not because anyone knows them in the sense of having derived them from other truths available to everyone.

This neat division between two kinds of truths concerning God—Thomas calls them, respectively, preambles of faith and mysteries of faith—is disturbed by the fact that the first sort of truth is either implicit or explicit in revelation. That is, among the things the believer believes about God are that God exists, that there is no more than one God, and other naturally knowable truths about God. Thomas accepts this as the case without thinking that it jeopardizes the absolute distinction between knowledge and faith. To know a truth is, by and large, to be able to show that it is true by appealing to other things whose truth is not in doubt. To believe a truth is to hold it as true on the authority of God's revelation. If both preambles and mysteries have been revealed, it follows that not everything that has been revealed is of faith, that some of the truths about God that we hold on the authority of revelation can come to be known. The larger part of revealed truths cannot become objects of knowledge in this sense; nonetheless, the fact that some can is not without significance. Indeed it provides the basis for an argument on behalf of the reasonableness of accepting as true what one does not understand. If some of the things God has revealed can come to be known to be true, it is reasonable to accept the rest, the mysteries, as in themselves intelligible, however obscure they must remain for us in this life. It will be noticed that this argument on behalf of the reasonableness of faith is not an effort to *prove* the truth of the mysteries.

This relation between preambles and mysteries, which preserves their difference, is carried over into the comparison of philosophy and theology. Philosophy takes its rise from common experience and from truths in principle accessible to anyone. Theology, on the other hand, has its starting point in truths that God has revealed about Himself. What distinguishes theology from faith, according to Thomas, is that theology is a more or less sophisticated reflection on believed truths that brings to bear on them whatever we know from other sources. This is the sense of the traditional view that philosophy is the handmaid of theology. Philosophy, that is, all natural knowledge, is used by the theologian in his attempts to understand what he believes.

These considerations may suffice to indicate why it is that we encounter so very much philosophical speculation in the theological works of Thomas Aquinas. It is not simply that he had ready to hand philosophical truths that he then brought to bear on the faith. That was sometimes the case, but often he found it necessary to develop the philosophical base he needed in order to reflect on the mysteries of faith.

Thomas's concession that the preambles as well as the mysteries are included in revelation raises an obvious question: Why did God reveal truths about Himself that men are capable of knowing, that is, of finding out for themselves? The answer that Thomas develops in response to this question gives us a better idea of what He is and is not claiming for philosophical or natural theology. While holding that some knowledge of God, some truths about God, are attainable independently of revelation, Thomas stresses that it is knowledge that can be reached only after a long time and with a great deal of effort and an admixture of error. Man's mind has been darkened by sin, original and actual, and it is no easy matter for him to achieve knowledge about God even though in principle it is within his grasp. Yet knowledge of God, conviction that there is a God and that He is as He is, is of massive importance for human life. It may not be true that if God does not exist anything is permitted, but surely we would lead different lives as atheists than we do as theists and as Christians. The fact that God has revealed naturally knowable truths about Himself suggests that, if He had not, it is highly unlikely that we would be clear about them and yet more unlikely that many people would attain them.

This has even more particular consequences in the moral order as Thomas views it. We saw him speak of the human good as philosophers describe it as imperfect happiness. The fact is that men are now called to a perfection that transcends anything commensurate with human nature. The Beatific Vision is not something owed us because of the kind of creature we are. We are called to a happiness it would not have entered the mind of man to imagine. Our elevation to the supernatural life, thanks to the grace won by Christ by his redemptive act, completely alters our conception of the point and meaning of our lives.

Just as there are certain naturally knowable truths concerning God that we are nonetheless unlikely to achieve, so there is an imperfect happiness possible of attainment in this life but one nevertheless that few men are likely to attain. Perfect happiness, union with God, is an end we are incapable of achieving without that special help of God called grace. Natural theology, it paradoxically turns out, is best carried on within the ambience of the faith. So too, naturally knowable truths about how we should behave as men are sustained and bolstered by religious faith.

It is obvious what happens to the great truths about human action when they have nothing but a humanistic context to sustain them. In our own time, the role of the Church in keeping us clear on such matters as abortion and the demands of sexual morality is manifest. When argument falters, we need the support of belief, and in the absence of faith the arguments seldom get formed or are badly formed and confusion abounds.

That there is a striking parallel in the moral order to the preambles of faith in the speculative order is not always noticed. When Thomas discusses the Decalogue, he remarks that almost all the

Ten Commandments are truths about action that are naturally knowable. Indeed, he says that they are by and large precepts of natural law. Is it not then surprising that such practical truths should have been revealed by God? Obviously, it is far more surprising than is the case with the preambles of faith. Any speculative truths about God would be arrived at only after all sorts of other things have become known; the knowledge of truths about God presupposes knowledge of a great many other truths. But, although natural law precepts are starting points, not points of arrival, yet some have been revealed by God in the Tablets of the Law. Why?

Thomas holds that we have been more wounded by sin in the moral order than in the intellectual order. The lives we lead can cloud our minds, with the result that there is confusion about principles that are all but self-evident. To remedy this, we need grace to illumine our minds and to strengthen our wills if we are to achieve even the imperfect happiness recognized by pagan philosophers.

Of course the function of grace is not simply to enable us to attain our natural end but to provide us with the indispensable means of attaining our supernatural end, loving union with God for eternity. This is why Thomas will speak of virtues other than those that are acquired by repeated acts of the same kind. That is, there are infused virtues as well. Faith, Hope, and Charity are theological virtues that are gifts of God. There are infused moral virtues as well.

> It should be said that through virtue man is perfected with respect to the acts whereby he is ordered to happiness. . . . There is, however, a twofold happiness or felicity of man as was said above. One which is proportioned to human nature, which man can attain by the principles of his nature; another a happiness which exceeds the nature of man, which man can attain only through a participation in divinity, as it is said in the Second Epistle of Peter, 1:4, that through Christ we are made sharers in the divine nature. (ST IaIIae, q. 62, a. 1, c)

Without grace, the human agent cannot avoid serious sin. Thomas allows that men could without grace achieve virtue as the philosophers understand it, but now he wants to say that such acquired virtues are not virtues in the full sense. They are virtues only in a manner of speaking, because they do not order man to his true ultimate end. That is what the infused virtues do; accordingly they are virtues without qualification. A further mark of the infused virtues is that they cannot be lost by a single contrary action, something that is not the case with acquired virtues.

Needless to say, Thomistic moral theology is another and most complicated story. The preceding remarks are meant only to indicate that there is that further story and that it contains features that cast new light on the story we have tried to tell, that of Thomas's teachings in the area of moral philosophy.

The problem of morality is both a cognitive and an existential one. That is, we must both know what it is we ought to do and then act in accord with that knowledge. The problem becomes an enduring puzzle when it is recognized that someone can know what he ought to do and yet fail to act as he knows he should. This is not something the moral philosopher can easily accept. Surely, there must be some defect in such knowledge; if one does not do the right thing, this is because he does not *really* know what the right thing to do is. To hold otherwise seems to call into question the primacy of reason.

Well, we saw earlier how Thomas handles the issues this difficulty involves. What the difficulty threatens is not the claim that man is a rational animal but rather certain understandings of that characterization of man. We use our reason in many ways, ways that vary because of the things thought about and the purposes for which we undertake to reason. If reasoning is thought of only in its mathematical modes and human action is held to be reasonable in that sense, strange demands will be made on agents, strange and unmeetable demands, and, when it is seen that they cannot be met, the tendency will be to say that action is not rational or reasonable.

In the foregoing pages I have tried to present the moral philosophy of St. Thomas in such a way that it can be seen as flowing from his conception of man as a rational agent. This for Thomas is the peculiar mark of the human agent, that he puts his mind to what he does and consciously directs himself to the goods he recognizes as fulfilling of him. That is the starting point: the human person choosing and deciding in the myriad and fluctuating circumstances of life. The overriding question of moral philosophy thus becomes: How can we do well what we are already doing, what we cannot not do, namely, engage in conscious deliberate activity?

From the nature of the human agent so considered we can formulate great nongainsayable truths about the human good. Such truths are implicit in any particular decision; their articulation is of value since they suggest that, despite the contingency and continuous alteration of the circumstances in which we act, despite the historical changes that make one century so different from another, there are absolutes of human action: some goods that will ever be constitutive of the human moral ideal, some kinds of action that are always destructive of the human good. This is the conviction that Thomas develops in his theory of natural law.

The certainty of such natural law principles is bought at a cost, however. In order to be absolute they must, as the word suggests, be freed from those altering conditions. But it is only in concrete circumstances that men act, and we expect of the moral philosopher advice more tailored to the realm of action. We need more informative rules, counsel that is not so general. And we receive it. We find quite circumstantial rules enunciated by moral philosophers, enshrined in moral codes, parts of legal systems. But this greater informativeness is bought at a cost. Such rules do not apply always and everywhere. The agent must decide when they are applicable, how they are applicable, and all the rest. To the degree that moral philosophy is more and more helpful, to that degree it becomes less sure, more likely to seem quaint and inapplicable with the passage of time.

Thus, ultimately, the generalized reflection that is moral philosophy must be appropriated by singular agents and made to fit the here and now. We saw how Thomas viewed this process, speaking of the practical syllogism, insisting that reason works here in a mode that differs from its mode in moral philosophy, let alone in speculative disciplines. For the general to be made singular involves a cognitive problem, to be sure, but something is presupposed if the cognition is to arrive at its term. The reason embodied in action is under the influence of the agent's character. If the bent of appetite conflicts with what on the level of generality I know I should do, the problem of application cannot be solved by further argument.

This is hardly a surprise; it points to something we all already knew. When we begin to reflect about action, we are prepared to change our minds. But our ultimate objective is to change our lives. We become the kind of doer we should be by doing as we ought. The only way to learn to play the harp is to play the harp. Moral philosophy is thus of restricted utility. But one of its most useful lessons is that the kind of thought that goes into moral philosophy is not the kind that is identical with virtue. Arguments are nice, and we need them in doing moral philosophy. In order to change our lives, to become what we ought to be, we must perform repeated acts of the same kind, first against our grain, perhaps, then with less and less resistance, until finally we do joyfully and with pleasure the right thing.

When we reach that point we will have become the sort of person of whom Aristotle speaks. In questions of the human good, of what ought to be done, the good man is the measure.

Bibliographical Note

There are many general works and surveys a reading of which would enhance the usefulness of this book. I will mention Jacques Maritain, *Moral Philosophy* (New York: Scribner's, 1964), Vernon Bourke, *A History of Ethics* (New York: Doubleday, 1964), and Alasdair Macintyre, *A Short History of Ethics* (New York: Macmillan, 1966). See as well Servais Pinckaers, O.P., *The Sources of Christian Ethics,* translated by Sr. Mary Thomas Noble, O.P. (Washington: The Catholic University of America Press, 1995); Thomas S. Hibbs, *Dialectic and Narrative: An Interpretation of the Summa Contra Gentiles* (Notre Dame: University of Notre Dame Press, 1995); Alasdair MacIntyre, *Three Rival Forms of Moral Enquiry* (Notre Dame: University of Notre Dame Press, 1990); Jean Porter, *The Recovery of Virtue* (Louisville: Westminster/John Knox Press, 1990); John Finnis, *Fundamentals of Ethics* (New York: Fordham University Press, 1983); and Brian Davies, *The Thought of Thomas Aquinas* (Oxford: The Clarendon Press, 1992). The seminal work for Anglo-American ethics of this century is G. E. Moore's *Principia Ethica* (Cambridge: Cambridge University Press, 1903). Almost as important are R. M. Hare's *The Language of Morals* (Oxford: Clarendon Press, 1952) and *Freedom and Reason* (Oxford: Clarendon Press, 1963). See Philippa Foot's anthology *Theories of Ethics* (London: Oxford University Press, 1967). See too Henry B. Veatch, *For An Ontology of Morals* (Evanston: Northwestern University Press, 1971) and Ronald Lawler's *Philosophical Analysis and Ethics* (Milwaukee: Bruce Publishing Co., 1968), as well as Patrick McGrath's *The Nature of Moral Judgment* (Notre Dame: University of Notre Dame Press, 1969). Recent books of peculiar importance are Alan Donagan's *The Theory of Morality* (Chicago: University of Chicago Press, 1977), and Alasdair MacIntyre's *After Virtue* (Notre Dame: University of Notre Dame Press, 1980). Of continuing interest is John A. Oesterle's *Ethics* (Englewood Cliffs: Prentice Hall, 1957).

The main source for this book is the First Part of the Second Part of St. Thomas Aquinas's *Summa theologiae,* but I have usually had on the edge of my mind his *Commentary on Aristotle's Nichomachean Ethics* as well. An English translation of the latter by C. I. Litzinger was reissued by Dumb Ox Books (Notre Dame, Indiana) in 1993. A translation of *the Disputed Question on Evil* by John and Jean Oesterle will soon be published by the University of Notre Dame Press.

CHAPTER 1

"Nam idem sunt actus morales et actus humani": "for moral acts and human acts are the same thing," *ST* IaIIae, q. 1, a. 3, c. (This will be my way of citing: decoded it reads *Summa theologiae,* First Part of the Second Part, Question One, Article Three, body of the article. 2m where c occurs will mean the answer to the second objection.) The distinction between performing a certain skill well and performing well without qualification can be found, for example, in IaIIae, q. 57. Being good at an art or science is not the same thing as being a good man in the moral sense. Thomas has a lively sense of the role of the fortuitous in human affairs. The implications of this for the moral life are touched on in IaIIae, q. 6, a. 8, and q. 20, a. 5.

CHAPTER 2

The usual objections to Aristotle can be found in W. F. R. Hardie, *Aristotle's Ethical Theory* (Oxford: Clarendon Press, 1968). A good recent anthology is that of Amelie Oksenberg Rorty, *Essays on Aristotle's Ethics* (Berkeley: University of California Press, 1980). A sympathetic demur can be found in Bernard Williams, *Morality: An Introduction to Ethics* (New York: Harper and Row, 1972). Williams makes good use of the brilliant piece by Peter Geach, "Good and Evil," which can be found in Geach's *God and the Soul* (London: Routledge and Kegan Paul, 1969).

CHAPTER 3

A discussion of practical reason can be found in Yves Simon, *Critique of Moral Knowledge,* translated by Ralph McInerny (Notre Dame: University of Notre Dame Press, 1997). The literature on natural law is vast. See John Finnis, *Natural Law and Natural Rights* (Oxford: Clarendon Press, 1980), for itself alone, for its use of the work of Germain Grisez, and for its bibliography. With Russell Shaw, Grisez wrote *Beyond the New Morality* (Notre Dame: University of Notre Dame Press, 1974). Grisez's "The First Principle of Practical Reason" may be found in *Aquinas: A Collection of Critical Essays,* ed. Anthony Kenny (Garden City: Anchor Books, 1969). See E. B. F. Midgley, *The Natural Law Tradition and the Theory of International Relations* (New York: Barnes and Noble, 1975). See generally *The American Journal of Jurisprudence* (formerly *The Natural Law Forum*), published by the Notre Dame Law School under the editorship of Robert Rhodes and Charles Rice. The quotations from Philip Devine and Eric D'Arcy in this chapter are from Philip Devine, *The Ethics of Homicide* (Ithaca: Cornell University Press, 1978), and Eric

D'Arcy, *Conscience and Its Right to Freedom* (New York: Sheed and Ward, 1961).

CHAPTER 4

The discussion of voluntary, involuntary, and non-voluntary is little more than a paraphrase of IaIIae, q. 6. On the matters discussed in the second part of the chapter, see Alan Donagan's "St. Thomas on the Analysis of Human Action," in *The Cambridge History of Later Medieval Philosophy*. See now Ralph McInerny, *Aquinas on Human Action* (Washington: The Catholic University of America Press, 1992).

CHAPTER 5

The references to Thomas are given in the text. Abelard's work has been edited and translated by D. E. Luscombe, *Peter Abelard's Ethics* (Oxford: Clarendon Press, 1971).

CHAPTER 6

Alasdair MacIntyre's *After Virtue: A Study in Moral Theory* (Notre Dame: University of Notre Dame Press, 1981) is a contemporary position not dissimilar to Thomas's.

CHAPTER 7

Josef Pieper's work on prudence is in *The Four Cardinal Virtues* (Notre Dame: University of Notre Dame Press, 1966).

For the rest, the presentation is adequately documented in the text. On some of the matters discussed in Chapter 8, the reader may wish to consult my *Saint Thomas Aquinas* (Boston: Twayne, 1977), reissued in paperback by the University of Notre Dame Press. A book in the same style as this is my *A First Glance at Thomas Aquinas: A Handbook for Peeping Thomists* (Notre Dame: University of Notre Dame Press, 1990).

Index